LEADERSHIP SIDEWAYS
by Gibson Sylvestre

LEADERSHIP SIDEWAYS:

Copyright © 2010 by Gibson Sylvestre
All rights reserved.

Requests for information should be addressed to:
P.O. Box 934741
Margate, FL 33093

Website: www.gibsonsylvestre.com

Printed in the United States of America.

Cover design by Aja Wilson

Layout design by Michele Scanlan

All rights reserved. No part of this book shall be reproduced, stored in a retrieval system, or transmitted by any means without written permission from the author.

ISBN: 978-0-578-04150-6

Presented To:

The Honorable Minnijean Brown-Trickey

From:

Gibson Sylvester

On:

January 17th, 2020

Thank you for your service!!! You have been a HUGE inspiration to me!!! Let's stay in touch
gibson@gibsonsylvestre.com

OTHER LIFE-CHANGING BOOKS BY GIBSON SYLVESTRE

ONLY $15 LIFE On PURPOSE: Allow God to ignite His passion and purpose in you! ISBN: 978-0-615-21166-4
Life On Purpose, Gibson's long awaited book is on its way to becoming a best-seller. Many around the world have been touched by this book! In this book Gibson shares sound biblical principles on connecting with God and discovering your purpose. This no-nonsense book will help you dream big as you lend a helping hand to others. Reflecting much of Gibson's spoken-word spontaneity, humor, and passion, Life On Purpose is written for the 21st Century Man or Woman who seeks to stand out of the crowd and CHANGE THE WORLD!
To Purchase Go To: www.GibsonSylvestre.com

ONLY $26.95 Supersize Your Life
ISBN:978-0-578-01878-2
In Super Size Your Life you'll learn how to strategically accomplish more in life. Through the wisdom gathered from years of research and interviews with successful business leaders and community influencers this book will help you reach the next level of success! Learn how to "supersize your life" as you learn critical lessons from people like Rosa Parks, Lou Holtz, Martin Luther King, Jr., Stephen Covey, John F. Kennedy and many others.
To Purchase Go To: www.GibsonSylvestre.com

ONLY $26.95 Staying Positive In A Negative World
ISBN: 978-0-578-01879-9

In a world full of negativity, Staying Positive in a Negative World will help you navigate through daily life with a positive and winning attitude. The transformational words written in this book will help you possess unshakable optimism, aid you to defeat your giants and challenge you to make a difference in this world! Learn how to 'stay positive in this negative world' as you learn ground-breaking lessons from people like Ralph Waldo Emerson, Mark Twain, Martin Luther King, Jr., Maya Angelo, William Shakespeare, U.S. President Franklin D. Roosevelt and Gibson Sylvestre who said, "Life is not about what you can get, but rather what you can give!"

To Purchase Go To: www.GibsonSylvestre.com

ONLY $59.99 Being A Promotable Person
ISBN: 978-0-578-03784-4

Being A Promotable Person will challenge you to look at work not as a frantic stumbling block but a friendly stepping stone to a life filled with meaning and purpose. Jim Collins, author of *Good To Great*, said, "It is impossible to have a great life unless it is a meaningful life. And it is very difficult to have a meaningful life without meaningful work." I want to encourage you to embark on the journey of searching for a deeper meaning. Don't settle for less. This book is about empowering you to achieve your highest God-given potential. This book is about maximizing every work moment and making them magnificent. Being a Promotable Person will help you work with a compelling sense of purpose by directing you to create a personal mission statement for your work. A 2008 Salary.com survey revealed 73% of participants admitted they spent part of their work day on activities that were not work-related at all. *Being A Promotable Person* will help you harness the power of focus.

To Purchase Go To: www.GibsonSylvestre.com

DEDICATION

I would like to dedicate this book to you, the reader. I want you to lead courageously and become a transformational leader.

Ode To My Mentor

This is my ode to my mentor that's owed my mentor...

There can be no successful lawyer without a mentor who first succeeded at being a great listener and patient teacher.

There can be no great leader without the leader succeeding at being a great follower.

A good leader is like a candle, he consumes himself while lighting the path for others to follow.

Thank you for giving me the blessing of learning from you,
Thank you for turning my inquisitiveness into insightfulness,
And my inexperience into inspiration mixed with information.
This ode is to my mentor because it's owed my mentor...

It's been said that a man's strength is not measured by how high he climbs
But how high he lifts up others and helps them rise.
Thanks for lifting me higher to reach my dreams, to achieve the prize.
This ode is to my mentor because it's owed my mentor...

I know my sentiments of gratitude is overdue,
And as my dad used to say, "Never wait until the grave to say, 'Thank You!'"
So this is my moment allow me to say it,

"Thank You!"
By: Gibson Sylvestre

ACKNOWLEDGMENTS

I would like to thank all of the leaders in my life that have helped me become the leader I am today, I really appreciate all that you do and all that you have done.

I would like to thank my beautiful, wonderful bride Brigitte for her assistance in editing this book. Brigitte is my soul mate and I am eternally grateful to her!

Special thanks to Michele Scanlan for her outstanding work on the editing and layout of this book. Michele is a servant-leader and a vital part of our team.

Special thanks to Aja Wilson for her leadership and expertise in the creative arts.

Brigitte, Michele, and Aja, without your help this book would not be possible.
Thanks!

TABLE OF CONTENTS

1. The Purpose-Driven Leader 1
2. Leaders Admit That They're Human 17
3. Leaders Communicate Strategically 29
4. Affirm Them to Greatness 41
5. Leaders Serve Others 55
6. Share The Leadership 69
7. Leaders Know When To Recharge Their Batteries 87
8. Lead With Courage 101

Epilogue 114

About the Author 116

HOW TO GET THE MOST OUT OF THIS BOOK

1) Read each chapter twice before moving to the next chapter.

2) Teach what you've learned from this book to someone else. The best form of learning is teaching what you've learned to others.

3) Highlight important concepts and principles within this book.

4) Write your thoughts in the margins.

5) Do the practical exercises and make them become a regular part of your daily routine.

6) Be generous with this book. Give copies of this book to those you know could benefit from it.

7) Master the principles in this book.

MY LEADERSHIP COVENANT

I,_____,
understand that I am undertaking an intensive, purpose-driven journey directed towards becoming a transformational leader. I am committed to this journey. I take full responsibility for my personal growth. I commit to reading and applying these life-changing principles to my everyday life. I understand that practically practicing these principles will enhance my life as well as the lives of those around me. I am 100% committed to practicing the principles of servant-leadership. I will serve others and lead them courageously.

_____   _____
Your Signature   Date

_____   _____
Witness Signature   Date

PREFACE

Where have the leaders gone? Are there any men and women of character left? Where are the modern day Patrick Henrys, who at the brink of the American Revolution cried, "Give me liberty or give me death!" This was a man of great conviction. Today, is your cry 'give me transformational leaders or give me death?' Are you a person of great conviction? Do you buckle under pressure? The type of leaders this desperate world is yearning for is not a leader who changes his or her tune with every whim of the wind. The leader who will prevail in the Twenty-first Century must be a person of great courage, great conviction, great humility, and great grit. The world is in desperate need of transformational servant-leaders. General H. Norman Schwarzkopf got it right when he said, "Leadership is a potent combination of strategy and character. But if you must be without one, be without strategy." What are your convictions? What will you stand by? **What will you die by?** Today, it's becoming increasingly popular for leaders to boast about "not holding any specific position." Everyone wants to be a leader, but nobody wants to sacrifice. Lately, I've been looking at all the events going on in the world and I've been deeply saddened by the lack of leadership. I find myself asking where have all the leaders gone? Are they all out to lunch? Are they sleeping? Have they died with history? Fundamentally, I believe that there are still great leaders out there they just need to be summoned. As the Chinese say, "When the student is ready the teacher will appear." Don't wait any longer...here is your call. Your family, your organization, and this world need you to lead...right now! The call is urgent.

Great leaders assume their position of leadership cautiously and carefully. Those who cavalierly assume a leadership role are self-delusional and do not have a clue of what it really means to be a true leader. This type of leader doesn't last very long. World peace activist Bishop Desmond Tutu put it this way, "I am a leader by default, only because nature does not allow a vacuum." How true! Because we lead people we should do so with humility, honor, and with a tremendous sense of personal responsibility. Former U.S. President John Quincy Adams once said, "If your actions inspire others to dream more, learn more, do more and become more, you are a leader." Leadership is a privilege. **Leadership is a gift from on high and from the people who give you the permission to lead them.** Leadership is about serving the people you lead, not seeking to be served. Leaders enable others to succeed. They give others the necessary tools to become peak performers. They slow down and listen to what others are saying. They move beyond the verbal and are able to gaze into the eternal soul. Leadership is about bringing the best out of others. "Leadership is getting someone to do what they do not want to do in order to achieve what they want to achieve," says Hall Of Fame NFL coach Tom Landry.

Leadership Sideways shares timeless principles of what it takes to be a transformational leader. Robert Quinn says that the best leaders are transformative, which means that they are **enormously demanding** and yet **enormously caring** at the same time. *Leadership Sideways* is a thought provoking book that will challenge you to reconsider, reevaluate, and rediscover your assumptions about leadership. *Leadership Sideways* looks at leadership as "the great balancing act." We have to be so many things simultaneously while avoiding extremes. "The challenge of leadership is to be strong, but not rude; be kind, but not weak; be bold, but not bully; be thoughtful, but not lazy; be humble, but not timid; be proud, but not arrogant; have humor, but without folly," says Richard DeVos, American entrepreneur and owner of the Orlando Magic basketball franchise.

Leadership Sideways will teach you to be a leader instead of a lid, the head person and not the headache, the motivating manager not a menace. Leadership Sideways is about **becoming a leader that is worth following.** As leadership expert John C. Maxwell says, "People buy into the leader before they buy into the vision." If you were a follower, would you follow you? If you practice and internalize the principles in this book you will become a leader people will be lining up to follow. Maybe you feel stagnant in your growth as a leader. This book is designed to help you go from stagnation to stunning growth! *Leadership Sideways* will get you going and get you growing! *Leadership Sideways* will teach you the secrets of having a compelling vision that will help you work on your business not in your business. Great leadership is tying your success with your team's success to create a win-win scenario.

Leadership Sideways communicates the fundamental principle that leadership is about sacrificing for the sake of others. For example, the story is told of a World War II commander searching for a dangerous German platoon. As they approached the location it was nightfall so the commander ordered his men to set up camps in the woods and wait to attack in the morning.

In the morning they awoke to find the field was covered with snow and hidden explosives. If they traveled backwards, they would be captured by their enemies. They had no other alternative but to move forward. In a very sober tone the commander told his troops that someone would have to risk it all and walk across the snow covered field filled with bombs, to make a path for the rest of the platoon. If one man gets blown up another soldier would have to walk in his tracks, pick up where he left off and take a different route to get to the other side. Seconds later the commander started walking across the bomb covered field. Immediately, one of the young soldiers grabbed him and said, "Commander you cannot go first! If you die, who will be our leader?" The commander looked at the young zealous soldier and said, "Well I guess you will." Then he proceeded to walk across the field. Most of the soldiers squeezed their eyes shut as they prayed in silence, hoping for a miracle. Some cried, others just watched nervously, knowing that at any second their beloved leader could perish with one tiny misstep. Miraculously, the commander got to the other side and yelled, "Men! Follow my footsteps and you will make it to the other side...I MADE IT!" Essentially, this story communicates the essence of transformational leadership. Leadership is about taking people to the other side safely. In order to be transformative leaders we must first be sacrificial. Our motto should be, "Sacrificial service, not self-service." Our leadership needs the visionary prowess of Steve Jobs, the moral strength of Desmond Tutu, the electricity and charisma of John F. Kennedy, the alertness and resolve of Winston Churchill, and the gentleness, kindness, and compassion of Mother Teresa; that is what *Leadership Sideways* is all about!

> "People want to follow a leader that is going somewhere. If you are the leader, where are you leading your people to? If the leader is stagnant then the people will be stagnant as well. The fact of the matter is, 'you cannot follow a parked car.'"
> – Gibson Sylvestre

> "Management is efficiency in climbing the ladder of success; leadership determines whether the ladder is leaning against the right wall."
> – Stephen R. Covey, Leadership expert

1
THE PURPOSE-DRIVEN LEADER

As a leader what drives you? What gets you going? Where are you going? Some leaders live their lives on autopilot. They simply drift through life meandering through the maze of mediocrity. Purpose-driven leaders are electrifying and they carefully chart their way to purpose and victory. What drives your leadership team? What drives your frontline people? What is your overarching purpose? Transformational leaders lead with purpose and direction.

People want to follow a leader that is going somewhere. If the leader is stagnant then the people will be stagnant as well. The fact of the matter is, "you cannot follow a parked car." Sadly, many leaders are parked cars due to a lack of drive. Leaders know which direction they are going. Best-selling author and speaker Marcus Buckingham once said, "A leader's job is to rally people toward a better future." Leaders paint an exquisite picture for their current followers as well as potential followers. Do you know where you are going?

LEADERS MAKE SURE THEIR TEAM IS CLIMBING THE RIGHT LADDER

We are all climbing a ladder. However we must proceed with caution. Business leader and author Stephen R. Covey once said, "Management is efficiency in climbing the ladder of success; leadership determines whether the ladder is leaning against the right wall." Is your team climbing the right ladder? Hall of Fame Baseball player Yogi Berra put it this way, "You've got to be very careful if you don't know where you're going, because you might not get there." Yogi Berra's comment is humorous but it's true. Leaders must clarify the trajectory for their team. If the path is misty for you it will be murky for your followers. Leadership expert Max DePree was right when he said, "The first responsibility of a leader is to define reality. The last is to say thank you. In between the two, the leader must become a servant and a debtor. That sums up the progress of an artful leader." How true! How are you defining reality for your team? How are you building your people up? Where are you leading them?

THREE QUALITIES OF PURPOSE-DRIVEN LEADERS

Quality # 1 - They Have Ethos

People buy into the leader before they buy into his mission or vision. People accept the messenger before they accept his or her message. Transformative leaders practice healthy self-disclosure. Your followers want to know your story; it helps put things in context. Nothing happens inside a vacuum. Establish credibility with your constituents. Do this by telling them your story. Again, people buy into the leader before they buy into his or her mission.

Quality # 2 - They Believe In Their Mission

Having a keen sense of mission is contagious. People love to be around leaders who are passionate about their mission. Great leaders engender a compelling vision. Everyone wants to follow a leader who knows where he or she is going and loves where he or she is going. Consequently, no one wants to follow a leader who does not know where they are going. Give them a good reason why they should give their all to your organization. If

> *People love to be around leaders who are passionate about their mission.*

you cannot come up with a good reason why people should give your organization or company their absolute best, you are in trouble... big trouble. Leaders should indubitably have a compelling mission for their followers to follow and believe in.

Quality # 3 - They Develop Common Ground

Oprah Winfrey is a great example of a leader who knows how to establish common ground. She is considered one of the richest women on the planet today. Yet her main constituents are middle class women. Sounds like an anomaly huh? How is Oprah able to connect with so many people who are so different from her? How does a rich television celebrity make herself come across as one of the girls from the beauty salon? Oprah does not focus on what makes her different from her audience, she focuses on the similarities. When leaders focus on common grounds with followers, followers feel special...very special.

KNOW YOUR PURPOSE!

Ray Kroc, founder of McDonald's Corporation knew the importance of defining one's purpose. On one occasion while speaking to a group of college students someone asked Kroc, "Do you enjoy being in the burger business?" Ray Kroc's response was, "I'm not in the burger business I'm in the real estate business." In many cases Kroc would purchase prime locations to place his restaurants. Essentially, Kroc had devised a new strategy and purpose for his company. Kroc would lease or buy potential restaurant locations and then sell them as McDonald's franchises. His purpose was to get as many people into his business as possible to make hamburgers. Kroc's main responsibility was to procure prime locations and sell those locations in the form of franchises. Kroc's business strategy sought to create a win-win situation for all involved. The franchise owners would get what they wanted, which was a sense of ownership in a burgeoning company and Kroc would receive the necessary capital he needed to expand his company. Ray Kroc was a purpose-driven leader. This reminds me of something that happened when President John F. Kennedy visited the NASA headquarters and had an illuminating conversation with a man holding a mop. The president asked the man, "What do you do around here?" The custodian confidently held his head up and said, "I'm helping to put a man on the moon, Mr. President!" This is a classic example of a man who had a mission beyond his immediate job.

PEOPLE ARE HUNGRY FOR A SENSE OF PURPOSE

People are desperately searching for purpose. They are hungry for a cause greater than themselves. Everyone likes to

have a flag to salute. Everyone needs a mission to commit to. Ask yourself:
1. What is the flag of our particular organization?
2. What does our flag stand for?
3. Do my people know our cause?
4. Am I sending a clear message?
5. Am I boldly representing my flag?

Purpose is important. I would argue that purpose-driven leaders and companies have a huge competitive advantage over companies who simply drift through life. Renowned psychologist Abraham Maslow was famous for work in assessing human needs. Maslow connotes that once our physical needs have been satisfied we start to long for a deeper sense of meaning and definition. Maslow said that ultimately we are seeking "self-actualization" which I consider to be the same thing as purpose.

For psychiatrist and Holocaust survivor Viktor Frankl, having a sense of purpose literally saved his life. While in captivity, Frankl observed that the people who believed their lives had meaning and purpose beyond the suffering and torture had greater chances of survival in the concentration camps, beyond those who had given up all hope.

Likewise, leaders who lead with a definite purpose distribute life throughout their teammates and company. Conversely, leaders without a sense of purpose and definite direction hold their people back from

> **Leaders who lead with a definite purpose distribute life throughout their teammates and company.**

having a compelling sense of purpose. And when the people within an organization lack purpose the organization itself lacks purpose. Customers and constituents prefer to conduct business with a company that has a sense of purpose. Successful companies keep this idea front and center of everything they do: teams work more effectively if united by a common cause or purpose. Respected businesswoman, Mary Kay Ash, once declared, "We must have a theme, a goal, a purpose in our lives. If you don't know where you're aiming, you don't have a goal. My goal is to live my life in such a way that when I die, someone can say, she cared." Every company needs a cause. Every man needs a mission.

> **Teams work more effectively if united by a common cause or purpose.**

Having clear objectives increase your chances of hitting your targets. The clearer your purpose the easier you will hit the target! Lack of clear objectives will lead to frustration and dissatisfaction. Management expert Steven Covey exhorts us to, "Begin with the end in mind." The leaders who will succeed in the Twenty-first Century are the leaders who lead with a clear purpose.

BEYOND MONEY

Yes, we all need to make money. Without money nothing in our world can function. However, Jim Collins, author of *Built to Last* and *Good to Great*, put it this way, "money is like blood – we all need it to function, however it is not our main purpose in life." If your main purpose is to make a profit or get a pay check, you will lack strategic direction and motivation. Ray

Kroc, founder of McDonald's Corporation, once said, "If you work just for money, you'll never make it, but if you love what you're doing and you always put the customer first, success will be yours." Every company needs a purpose that transcends making a profit. People commit themselves to "transcendence" not mere money-making transactions. When we get off track, leaders help us see the big picture. French author Antoine de Saint-Exupery once said, "If you want to build a ship, don't drum up people to collect wood and don't assign them tasks and work, but rather teach them to long for the endless immensity of the sea." In other word, leaders help us see beyond 'what' we're doing into 'why' we're doing. If you want a company that lasts for a short time focus on money, if you want a company that last for generations focus on a cause. You will need a purpose to make it through the difficult storms and seasons of your organization. **Making money is an outcome of work not the purpose of work.**

THE LEADER'S JOB IS TO COMMUNICATE PURPOSE AND TO ENLIST OTHERS

Steve Jobs, of Apple Computers, knows the power of purpose. He convinced John Sculley to leave Pepsi to come work for Apple. Jobs did not utilize compensation, comfort or convenience as a means to convince Sculley to leave a comfortable position at an established company. What was Job's unique selling proposition? You have guessed it, it was purpose. Jobs asked Sculley to embark on a journey with him to "change the world."

In fact, Jobs told Sculley that all he was doing at Pepsi was manufacturing more and more "sugar water." Jobs told Sculley that if he joined him at Apple, he would have the unique opportunity to transform the world by transforming the way people learn and communicate through technology. Sounds like a compelling mission huh? It doesn't surprise me that Sculley left his security at Pepsi for an exciting mission at Apple.

Sculley's story sends a provocative message to all of us leaders. What's the message? **"Most people would rather follow a compelling purpose than remain comfortable!"**

PURPOSE WARMS HEARTS

Herb Kelleher, CEO of Southwest Airlines, always had a vision to have a company where "kindness and the human spirit are nurtured, where you do what your customers want and are happy in your work." Kelleher's mission was to have fun and be productive at the same time.

Herman Miller's former chairman, Max DePree called his people to a higher cause. Some might say they're just a furniture company. However, DePree had something else in mind. DePree told his people that they have a greater mission and purpose. Here's what he'd say, "My goal is that people look at us... not as a corporation, but as a group of people working intimately within a covenantal relationship, they'll say, 'These folks are a gift to the spirit.'" Pretty audacious words for an executive, huh? J. Kermit Campbell, the chairman that followed DePree added to the mission by saying that the purpose of their company was not to merely make products but to, "liberate the human spirit." Most people would love to work at theses companies because the leaders have found a purpose outside the mundane into the magnificent.

BRING THE TROOPS TOGETHER REGULARLY

Tom Chappell is the creator of the world's leading 'alternative toothpaste,' called Tom's of Maine. Chappell believes that his company expands far beyond producing toothpaste. Chappell brings all of his troops together once a month for a huge company sponsored party. They spend a half a day focusing on a specific aspect of their company's mission which includes "diversity, profitability, and conserving the environment." They spend approximately $75,000 in lost production time, "And it's worth every penny," says Chappell. During these meetings the company gathers a plethora of useful recommendations on how to improve their operation and be more efficient. In addition, these monthly meetings have proven to enhance teamwork, boost morale and show the employees that top management really cares. This investment of time and money helps the company replenish the emotional reserves of their employees. "When we need to call upon the reserves of our people — to dig in deeper, meet extraordinary goals — we can expect it here," says Chappell the company's CEO. The mission of the people of Tom's of Maine is not simply to make toothpaste, but to build the community and impact the world in positive ways.

> ... monthly meetings have proven to enhance teamwork, boost morale and show the employees that top management really cares.

VALUE YOUR VALUES

What are your overarching values? What do you want your company to stand for? These are important questions that demand serious soul searching. Hewlett-Packard keeps values at the forefront of the minds of its people. Emily Duncan, director of global diversity and work life for Hewlett-Packard elaborates on the power of having a common purpose. She says, "We have been fortunate at Hewlett Packard, because we have had the strength of the HP way to help us cope... It represents our deeply held values, shared practices, and policies that have always guided the company." What are their guiding principles? According to Duncan, Hewlett-Packard's guiding principles are "trust and respect for the individual, high achievement, uncompromising integrity, and teamwork." Notice how the employees are first and foremost loyal to the values of the company, not the founders or leadership of the company. Leaders make a big mistake when they seek loyalty from their teammates when they have not first given them values. Give them values first. When they are loyal to the values of the company only then can they be loyal to the leaders of the company.

> *...employees are first and foremost loyal to the values of the company...*

MERCK'S ON A MISSION

The goal of every business is to make a profit. Nobody goes into business and says, "I want to lose tons of money this year!" Anyone with that type of mentality would be considered

10 LEADERSHIP SIDEWAYS

absurd. However, when we make "making a profit" our only goal we set ourselves up for abysmal failure. **Successful companies have a combination of the desire to make a profit and the desire to make a difference.** That's exactly what Roy Vagelos, former chairman of Merck has done. Vagelos led the charge to develop Mectizan, medication utilized to cure river blindness or onchocerciasis, a disease found in the river regions of Africa. River blindness is caused by Onchocerca volvulus, a small parasitic worm contracted by a black fly bite. River blindness causes its victims to have crocodile skin, lesions, swelling, and ultimately, blindness. Many villages on the continent of Africa have been affected by this terrible disease.

The problem was most of the people who desperately needed this medication Merck manufactured could not afford to pay for it. Furthermore, Merck's policy said that they must discontinue research on any medication that earns $20 million or less in its first year. So did Merck stop manufacturing this medication? Did Merck chose profits over people? The answer is no! At the time the chairman of Merck, Mr. Vagelos decided to go against the grain and start a revolution of generosity. He decided to manufacture the medication and distribute it for free to the African villagers. Many people criticize pharmaceutical companies because it seems that their first objective is to make a profit and not help people. Vagelos and Merck improved the image of pharmaceutical companies dramatically. They put people first, not the money. This same spirit of altruism and generosity was found in Merck's founder George Merck, who said, "Medicine is for the people and not for profits. If you remember that, the profits will follow." That's why Merck introduced streptomycin to Japan four decades earlier which helped eliminate tuberculosis throughout the entire country. Again, Merck did this without making any profit. Now four decades later "It's no accident that Merck is the largest American pharmaceutical company in Japan today," says Vagelos. Merck is a stunning example of a prosperous company with a helping hand and a heart of compassion. They are leaving a legacy far beyond "making a profit." **What will your organization be remembered for?** How will your organization demonstrate care and compassion? The way you answer these questions will reveal if your leadership led people to greed or greatness... you decide.

STUDY GUIDE SECTION

KEY POINTS

While reading, What principles on being a purpose-driven leader stood out to you the most? Why?

_____

_____

_____

REAL LIFE APPLICATION: PUTTING THE PRINCIPLES AND LESSONS INTO ACTION!

How will you apply this new information to your personal life?

_____

_____

_____

What are some obstacles that get in the way of you becoming a purpose-driven leader? What are some practical steps you can take to help remove some of those obstacles?

_____

_____

_____

PRACTICAL APPLICATION EXERCISE

Step 1- Review your company's mission statement.

Step 2- Rewrite your company's mission statement in less than five words.

Step 3- Now write your company's mission statement with one word.

Step 4- Share your abbreviated mission statement with your entire staff.

_____

_____

_____

RATE YOURSELF

Overall, do you communicate your company's mission in a compelling way?

(Check One Box Below)

Poor	Below Average	Average	Satisfactory	Excellent
1	2	3	4	5
❏	❏	❏	❏	❏

I am strongly committed to promoting a compelling purpose for my people to follow.

(Check One Box Below)

Poor	Below Average	Average	Satisfactory	Excellent
1	2	3	4	5
❏	❏	❏	❏	❏

GROWING GOAL

Write down at least one goal/objective you have for becoming a purpose-driven leader:

_____

_____

_____

Stepping stone # 1

_____

_____

_____

Stepping stone # 2

_____

_____

_____

Stepping stone # 3

_____

_____

_____

"We need to build organizations that can fly without super-humans. In our super hero-CEO culture we sometimes make it seem that CEOs and other types of leaders are infallible. Big mistake! None of us are perfect."
— Gibson Sylvestre

"Experience is simply the name we give our mistakes."
— Oscar Wilde, Poet and author

2
LEADERS ADMIT THAT THEY'RE HUMAN

We need to build organizations that can fly without super-humans. In our super hero-CEO culture we sometimes make it seem that CEOs and other types of leaders are infallible. Big mistake! None of us are perfect. Poet and author, Oscar Wilde said, "Experience is simply the name we give our mistakes." Making mistakes is unavoidable. Making mistakes is human. In this chapter I want to give you permission to make mistakes. I am not advocating that you go out and make unintelligent decisions. However, what I am saying is: admit mistakes frequently and learn from them! Motivational teacher, Denis Waitley once said, "The only person who never makes mistakes is the person who never does anything." Just because we make mistakes doesn't mean our mistakes have to make us!

WHY SHOULD YOU ADMIT WHEN YOU ARE WRONG?

World-renowned speaker and author Nikki Giovanni once declared, "Mistakes are a fact of life. It is the response to error that counts." How does a leader respond to mistakes?
- Some leaders hide their mistakes. Hiding mistakes only makes the leader disingenuous. Eventually, you will be found out and when your people find out you will lose all credibility.
- Some leaders deny their mistakes. When you deny your mistakes you make yourself susceptible to repeating them. Face the brutal facts and change.
- Some leaders play the "blame game." The "blame game" gives you a false sense that the mistake is not your responsibility. When you neglect your responsibilities you injure your abilities.

Admitting when you are wrong:
1. Builds Trust With Your Constituents
Trust is one of the most important pillars of leadership. When you are honest about your mistakes your people will trust you.

2. Makes You More Human
Many leaders want people to think that they are perfect, that is why they feel the need to hide their mistakes. Admitting your mistakes takes you off the pedestal and puts you on level ground. I had a friend who used to say, "The only thing a man can do on a pedestal is fall."

3. Makes You More Approachable

Admitting your mistakes makes you more approachable. People will instantly connect with you. When you're approachable you dramatically increase your opportunities to influence others.

4. Strengthens Your Leadership Over Time

Over the long run, people will have more respect for you as you are honest with them. No one enjoys making mistakes. Nevertheless, leadership is a high risk sport, because one of the requirements of leadership is to make decisions without having all of the knowledge. Consequently, whenever you are making decisions without all of the information you are bound to make some mistakes. Author Wess Roberts put it this way, "Anyone who doesn't make mistakes isn't trying hard enough." Once you realize that it's okay to make mistakes you will take more risks. And the more risks you take, the more opportunities you have to succeed, as the founder of Walt Disney World used to say, "The greater the risks the greater the rewards." Risk being real and watch your leadership soar!

> *The more risks you take, the more opportunities you have to succeed.*

LEADERS MAKE MISTAKES ...AND IT'S OKAY!

I can't stress this enough, leaders need to be more open with their mistakes. Legendary leadership expert Jack Welch once said, "Everyone who's running something goes home at night and wrestles with the same fear: Am I gonna be the one who blows this place up?" We all need certainty in our chosen endeavors; however along with the certainty we have, we will have some uncertainty as well. "If you're not making mistakes, you're not taking risks, and that means you're not going anywhere. The key is to make mistakes faster than the competition, so you have more changes to learn and win," says John W. Holt, Jr. coauthor of "Celebrate Your Mistakes." The next time you're tempted to beat yourself up, pause and say to yourself, "All great leaders make mistakes. It's okay. What I need to do is learn from this mistake."

THE TOP TEN MISTAKES LEADERS MAKE AND HOW TO CORRECT THEM

Mistake #1 - They Focus on Tasks Rather Than Vision

One of the biggest mistakes a leader can make is to allow their vision to become myopic. When you take your eyes off the prize you doom yourself to confusion and stress. A leader's job is to monitor the organization's progress and see if the organization is staying on tract to its vision.

Correction: *Focus on the big picture. Delegate the details to others.*

Mistake #2 - They Don't Stimulate Intellectually

Great leaders always stimulate us with challenging ideas. Challenge your people to think beyond themselves. Ideas are what moves people and organizations to action. Take Apple for example. When John Sculley, Michael Spindler and Gil Amelio became the three successive CEOs of Apple in the early 90s, Apple didn't perform as well. They were stuck in a rut. When Steve Jobs returned Apple made a surging comeback. Steve Jobs helped take Apple to the next level. Steve Jobs helped create the iPod which revolutionized the way the world accesses music. Steve Jobs knew how to stimulate his team to innovate.

> **Great leaders always stimulate us with challenging ideas.**

Correction: *Stimulate your team to innovate. Great ideas are what cause people to move.*

Mistake #3 - They Don't Focus On Solutions

Focusing on your mistakes is one of the biggest mistakes a leader can make. In a room full of questions the person with the answers is the leader. Whenever a problem arises focus on the solution not the problem.

Correction: *A leader's job is to come up with solutions.*

Mistake #4 - They Don't Rekindle Morale And Momentum

The morale and momentum within an organization is very, very, fragile. It is always in constant need of maintenance and repair. Leadership expert John C. Maxwell once said, "When big mo is on your side, you can do no wrong. But when big mo isn't on your side, you can do no right." No leader can possibly keep morale and momentum up one hundred percent all the time but that shouldn't stop him or her from trying.

Correction: *Rekindle The Fires Of Morale And Momentum Frequently.*

Mistake #5 - They Mimic Others Rather Than Manifest Who They Are

You will operate at your best being you. Yes, we can all learn from experts, however don't try to be someone else. Be the best you that you can be. Whenever we try to be someone else it turns out to be a disaster. As the great scholar and cartoonist Dr. Seuss once said, "Today you are You, that is truer than true. There is no one alive who is Youer than You." **Correction**: *Be Yourself! You Will Lead The Best As You Stay True To Yourself.*

Mistake #6 - They Attack Individuals Rather Than the Person's Behaviors

As leaders, we should never attack someone's personality. We should confront the behavior not the person. When you attack people's personality they will either blow up at you or get extremely defensive. Correct others with gentleness and LOVE. **Correction:** *Always give others respect and dignity when correcting them.*

Mistake #7 - They Conclude Meetings Without A Map

Every meeting or counseling session should be concluded with clear cut action steps and directives. Never conclude a meeting without a plan of action or map. When you end conferences, retreats, appraisals, meetings, and counseling sessions without clear directives you negate the purpose

> **Never conclude a meeting without a plan of action or map.**

of the meeting in the first place.
Correction*: End every meeting with a clear plan of action...and follow through.*

Mistake #8 - They Try To Be Too Controlling

Whenever leaders try to control others they naturally get out of control. Leaders are supposed to give liberty to others, not incarcerate them. We are supposed to monitor those we lead, but not control them. Controlling other human beings is animalistic and criminal.
Correction*: Leaders should influence not control.*

Mistake #9 - They Stop Growing And Improving Themselves

If a leader is not growing he or she is rotting. One of the primary jobs of a leader is to commit himself to constant self-improvement. If you stop growing eventually people will stop following you.
Correction*: Great Leaders Commit Themselves To Constant Self-improvement.*

Mistake #10 - They Fail To Stay Current To The Needs Of Their People

Leaders must constantly keep a pulse on those they're leading. Always know what's going on in their world. Know their everyday frustrations. Know what motivates them. Know what their current needs are and how to help them. If you lose touch with the problems of your people they will think you don't care about them. And if they think you don't care they will eventually stop following you.

Correction: Study Your People, Know Their Problems And How To Solve Them

LEARN FROM YOUR MISTAKES

As a leader, you will be criticized. Some may even try to crucify you. Don't be surprised when it happens. In fact, you know you're making an impact when everyone tries to take shots at you. As a wise man once said, "Don't mind criticism. If it is untrue, disregard it; if unfair, keep from irritation; if it is ignorant, smile; if it is justified, it is not criticism –learn from it." Always seek to grow from constructive criticism. Founder of FedEx, Frederick W. Smith once said, "Leaders get out in front and stay there by raising the standards by which they judge themselves — and by which they are willing to be judged." Many leaders get bitter and bent out of shape by criticism. When someone criticizes you learn from it and move on. Dr. James R. Angell, president of Yale University was once asked what his secret was for lasting so long and being so successful as the president of Yale, he explained: "Grow antennae, not horns." In other words, don't get bitter get better! View your mistakes as teachers. British composer John Powell put it his way, "The only real mistake is the one from which we learn nothing."

> **When someone criticizes you learn from it and move on.**

STUDY GUIDE SECTION

KEY POINTS

While reading, What principles on admitting you're human stood out to you the most? Why?

_____

_____

_____

REAL LIFE APPLICATION: PUTTING THE PRINCIPLES AND LESSONS INTO ACTION!

How will you apply this new information to your personal life?

_____

_____

_____

What are some obstacles that get in the way of admitting your frailties? What are some practical steps you can take to help remove some of those obstacles?

_____

_____

_____

PRACTICAL APPLICATION EXERCISE

The next time you make a mistake don't cover it up. Come out in the open and say, "I was wrong, I'm SORRY."

_____

_____

_____

RATE YOURSELF

Overall, how often do you admit your mistakes and weaknesses to your team?
(Check One Box Below)

Poor	Below Average	Average	Satisfactory	Excellent
1	2	3	4	5
❑	❑	❑	❑	❑

I am strongly committed to admitting my mistakes and improving my weaknesses.
(Check One Box Below)

Poor	Below Average	Average	Satisfactory	Excellent
1	2	3	4	5
❑	❑	❑	❑	❑

GROWING GOAL

Write down at least one goal/objective you have for removing all masks and being as genuine and transparent as possible as a leader:

_____

_____

_____

Stepping stone # 1

_____

_____

_____

Stepping stone # 2

_____

_____

_____

Stepping stone # 3

_____

_____

_____

"Poor leaders open their ears and close their minds when they communicate. Average leaders open their ears and minds when they communicate. Great leaders open their ears, their minds, and their hearts when they communicate. All things being equal, the person with the best communication skills will win."
— Gibson Sylvestre

"60% of all management problems result from faulty communication."
— Peter Drucker, Leadership Expert

3
LEADERS COMMUNICATE STRATEGICALLY

Great leaders are great communicators. They plan their communication strategy carefully. The preparation of today will ensure the success of tomorrow. One time, President Abraham Lincoln was asked when he started preparing for his famous Gettysburg Address, arguably one the greatest speeches in American history. Lincoln answered, "My entire life." Like Lincoln, successful leaders meticulously plan their communication. Communication is action oriented. Break the word down: "commune" and "Ation or action." It can be viewed as "together action." Peter Drucker, one of the world's leadership experts once said, "60% of all management problems result from faulty communication." Wow! Now do you see the importance of good communication?

COMMUNICATE WITH ALL OF YOUR BEING

Poor leaders open their ears and close their minds when they communicate. Average leaders open their ears and minds when they communicate. Great leaders open their ears, their minds, and their hearts when they communicate. All things being equal, the person with the best communication skills will win. Great leaders learn to read in between the lines, they listen with their hearts. Have you been listening with your heart lately?

MEASURE HOW YOUR MESSAGE IS BEING RECEIVED

How do you measure how people comprehend what you say? What measuring stick do you use? Measuring what others hear is a critical part of communication. Not measuring how one's message is being received is one of the common mistakes leaders make. Great communicators seek understanding by asking clarifying questions. They also paraphrase and ask the other to verify if they have heard correctly.

> *Measuring what others hear is a critical part of communication.*

THE THREE VS OF COMMUNICATION

The three "Vs" of communication helps understand the importance of nonverbal communication. Here are the three elements:

1. 38% of communication is based on your vocal tone. The tone of your voice helps others decipher what you are saying.

2. 7% of your communication is based on the "verbal" aspects of your conversation. This is the actual words you use.

3. 55% of your conversation is based on what you project visually. I call this nonverbal communication or body language. Over 93% of communication is nonverbal. Again, transformative leaders communicate with their vocal tone, verbal, and the visual presentation. Use this information to your advantage. Use all of the tools in your tool box to become a master communicator.

WHAT ARE THE PURPOSES OF COMMUNICATION?

Whenever you communicate you should have certain objectives in mind. Leaders use communication to:

1. **Educate**- What new information can you impart to your people? How can you educate your constituents in a fun and interesting way? Great leaders and communicators teach people in a dynamic way.

2. **Engage**- Great communication is always engaging. Leaders must captivate their constituents in order to influence them.

3. **Emote**- Great communicators emote or project their emotions in a positive way. This type of passion helps the leader to connect with his or her people emotionally.

WHAT IS THE MOST IMPORTANT TRAIT WHEN HIRING SOMEONE?

What do you think is the most important skill or trait when it comes hiring someone? Most people will say competence. However, the Wall Street Journal Corporate Recruiters Survey

tested 21 characteristics and attributes that are very important when it comes to hiring and here is what they found:
- 67.1 % Strategic Thinking
- 72.5 % Leadership Potential
- 74.5 % Fit in our corporate culture
- 82.9%Work Ethic
- 86.9% Integrity
- 89.0% Say Communication Skills Is The Most Important

As we can see communication is extremely important in the workplace. Great communication can help you close sales with major customers. It can help you in your personal life as well. Every area in your life will be enhanced by improving your communication skills.

COMMUNICATION AT THE SPEED OF LIGHT...

Today, communication is coming at us faster than ever before. We are bombarded with thousands of advertisements and solicitations on a daily basis. D.K. Burlow in his study entitled The Process of Communication, states that the average American spends 70% of his or her active hours each day verbally communicating. In fact:

- According to Reuters Magazine... "In the last 30 years mankind has produced more information than in the previous 5,000."
- "The average American sees 16,000 advertisements, logos, and labels in a day."
- Historically, technical information has been estimated to double every two years; by 2010 it is predicted to double every 72 hours.

With all this information at our finger tips why aren't we better communicators? Why are so many of our companies plagued with miscommunication? The truth is we don't stop long enough to listen to others. Author Anais Nin says, "We don't see things as they are, we see them as we are." As leaders, in order to become master communicators we must realize that the importance of information is determined by the listener not the author.

SAY IT WITH LOVE

When leaders have to confront they communicate in a respectable way. Leaders should always ask, "If this conversation were recorded, would I be embarrassed if my spouse, children, and friends heard what I was saying? If you answer "yes" then you shouldn't be saying it.

> **When leaders have to confront they communicate in a respectable way.**

When confronting remember to:
1. Praise before you present your constructive criticism.
2. Confront in private. Praise in public!
3. Be very tactful. (Speak to them not at them.) Speak to them like you would want to be spoken to.

THREE CRITICAL LAWS OF COMMUNICATION

Communication is a critical part of leadership. Great leaders never stop improving their ability to communicate effectively. Here are the three critical laws of communication.

Number 1- THE LAW OF Simplicity

The best communicators keep things simple. Just think of how stamps help messages get to where they need to go. Simple communication helps teams communicate at a higher level.

Remember S.T.A.M.P. stands for:
- Simple
- Things
- Are
- More
- Precise

"You can have brilliant ideas, but if you can't get those ideas across, they don't do anybody any good," said Former Chrysler Corporation Chairman Lee Iacocca.

Number 2- THE LAW OF Seeking Understanding

Communication is a two-way street. Leaders seek to understand the other person's perspective before they seek to get their points across. Most people communicate simply to be heard. They only want to get their points across and ignore the other person's perspective. Great leaders are humble enough to hear another person's perspective even when they disagree with it.

Number 3- THE LAW OF Active Listening

People can listen four to ten times faster than they can speak. Listening is the cornerstone of effective communication. An old Sioux Native American saying declares, "If you

> **Listening is the cornerstone of effective communication.**

listen for the whispers you won't have to hear the screams." Are you listening to the whispers of your people? Listening means giving an ear to whoever is communicating. We use our ear to:

a) E = Explain- Leaders allow the other party to explain their point of view.

b) A = Acknowledge- Leaders acknowledge the feelings as well as the opinions of others.

c) R = Respond- Leaders respond to what their constituents are saying because they care about people.

Dr. James Lynch, co-director of the Psychophysiological Clinic and Laboratories at the University of Maryland has documented that an actual healing of the cardiovascular system takes place when we listen. Blood pressure rises when people speak and lowers when they listen. Listening has healing properties for the soul. Simply put, great leaders are listeners.

STUDY GUIDE SECTION

KEY POINTS

While reading, What principles on communicating strategically stood out to you the most? Why?

_____

_____

_____

REAL LIFE APPLICATION: PUTTING THE PRINCIPLES AND LESSONS INTO ACTION!

How will you apply this new information to your personal life?

_____

_____

_____

What are some obstacles that get in the way of you communicating effectively? What are some practical steps you can take to help remove some of those obstacles?

_____

_____

_____

PRACTICAL APPLICATION EXERCISE

Step 1- Reread the three laws of communication.

Step 2- Rewrite them on a blank sheet of paper.

Step 3- Memorize them.

Step 4- Use them as your guide for your next board meeting, staff meeting, or speech.

_____

_____

_____

RATE YOURSELF

Overall, how well do you strategically communicate as a leader?

(Check One Box Below)

Poor	Below Average	Average	Satisfactory	Excellent
1	2	3	4	5
☐	☐	☐	☐	☐

I am strongly committed to becoming a strategic communicator.

(Check One Box Below)

Poor	Below Average	Average	Satisfactory	Excellent
1	2	3	4	5
☐	☐	☐	☐	☐

GROWING GOAL

Write down at least one goal/objective you have for improving your communication skills:

_____

_____

_____

Stepping stone # 1

_____

_____

_____

Stepping stone # 2

_____

_____

_____

Stepping stone # 3

_____

_____

_____

JOURNAL ENTRY
Why is effective communication so important to a leader?

_____

_____

_____

_____

_____

"Why is it that most employees show more enthusiasm for their local bowling teams than they show for their 9 to 5 jobs? Could it be because they get a sense of appreciation and value at the bowling alley that they don't get at work? We need to affirm them."
— Gibson Sylvestre

"How do you know if a man needs encouragement? If he is breathing."
— S. Truett Cathy, Founder of Chick-Fil-A

4
AFFIRM THEM TO GREATNESS

Many leaders believe that giving their team affirmation and empowerment will take away from their leadership. Nothing can be further from the truth. They say things like, "If I give my assistant a compliment on her work she may start slacking off. They may think I'm weak if I go around spouting out encouragement. Giving affirmation won't affect my bottom line anyway. I simply don't have time to say nice little things to people...I'm just not good at it." Have you ever said any of those statements to yourself? Allow me to respond to these statements:

1. LIE: Compliments cause people to slack off in their work.
TRUTH: Compliments actually cause people to work harder. It shows them that you actually notice and appreciate their hard work.

2. LIE: Affirming and encouraging others will make you look weak.

TRUTH: When you affirm and encourage others you demonstrate your strength. Only small people are afraid to lift others up.

3. LIE: Giving affirmation won't affect your bottom line anyway.

TRUTH: Giving affirmation produces more engaged workers. Engaged workers produce better results. Better results equal a hefty bottom line.

4. LIE: You don't have time to say nice little things to people.

TRUTH: No matter what industry you are in if you are not nice to people you won't be in that industry very long. People like to do business with nice people. Period.

We only become even more powerful when we give our power away. The more you give the more you receive. Some of the best, larger-than-life leaders I know are the ones who empower others to reach their potential. Leaders liberate the leaders in their followers.

AFFIRMATION BRINGS OUT THE BEST IN OTHERS

Leaders believe in affirming others. Why is it that most employees show more enthusiasm for their local bowling teams than they show for their 9 to 5 jobs? Could it be because they get a sense of appreciation and value at the bowling alley that they don't get at work? We need to affirm them. People work harder in environments that breed appreciation.

> *People work harder in environments that breed appreciation.*

Affirmation brings out the best in others. Affirmation acknowledges the dignity in others. Everyone has something of value to offer. "Leadership is communicating people's worth and potential so clearly that they are inspired to see it in themselves," says leadership expert and best-selling author Stephen Covey. Through the years tremendous leaders have called me higher in my career. I can honestly say if it wasn't for the mentors and coaches in my life I don't think I could have made it. You have that same opportunity. Your people are waiting for you to give them a vision so intriguing and captivating that it lifts them up from a life of mediocrity to a life of mastery.

LEADERS ARE LIFTERS NOT LIDS

Again, one of the main purposes of leadership is to lift others up. "Too many leaders feel that their main job is making other people feel unimportant...," says leadership legend Ken Blanchard. Small leaders put others down to go up. Transformational leaders push people up to go up with them. Many leaders become very insecure about those that they are leading. So they do things to purposely sabotage the success of others. If you are insecure, shift your paradigm. Instead of thinking if your people are better equipped than you are they will take your place, look at it this way: if your people are more equipped than you, it only makes you look better. Remember, the primary job of a leader is to serve, not to be served.

CULTIVATE STRENGTHS NOT WEAKNESSES

Are your people allowed to take calculated risks? Have you given them the permission to make mistakes? Do you focus on your people's strengths or weaknesses? In his book Strengths Finder 2.0 Tom Rath sites the Gallup Research Poll which says that if a leader primarily focuses on ignoring i.e. not complimenting and affirming those that they lead, there's a 40% chance of their team being disengaged. If a leader focuses on the weaknesses of those they lead there is a 22% chance of their employees being disengaged at work. If a leader focuses on the strengths of their team there is only a 1% chance of a disengaged team. Do you see why giving encouragement and focusing on your people's strengths is so important?

> *Do you focus on your people's strengths or weaknesses?*

CRITERIA FOR POSITIVE REINFORCEMENT AND GOOD COACHING

Knowledge = What to do! Let your people know exactly what you want them to do. If you are unclear with your instructions your people will become frustrated and disengaged.

Skill = How to do it! Show them how to do it. Demonstration is a powerful coaching tool. Don't assume your people know how you want them to do things. If you don't know their specific skills, send them for some training. Your main goal is to make them an expert at what they do.

Attitude = The way to do it! Model a positive attitude for your people. Don't become a victim of doing the right things with the wrong attitude. If your people are doing things with the wrong attitude correct them immediately.

Action = Do it! There's a time for training and there's a time for action. You can have the world's greatest strategies but if you don't implement them they mean nothing!

CRITERIA FOR GIVING THE G.I.F.T OF AFFIRMATION

Every time you give someone an encouraging word you are giving them a valuable gift. Here is a formula that has been very beneficial to the leaders I coach:

"G" Is For Genuine

When you are affirming others make sure you speak from your heart. French theologian and philosopher Jacques Maritain once said, "Showing a genuine concern and respect for your work, your people and your community may be the best strategy in reaching your goal of outstanding leadership." When you are genuine you connect with the hearts of your people.

"I" Is For Informed

Don't put your head in the sand. Leaders must know what is going on in their organization. When you give a compliment or affirmation don't be general, be as specific as possible. "You need to be aware of what others are doing, applaud their efforts, acknowledge their successes, and encourage them in their pursuits. When we help one another, everybody wins," said Olympian Jim Stovall.

"F" Is For Face-to-face

I keep letters and correspondence I receive from leaders, because they mean a lot to me. Recently, I was blessed to receive a personal note from my friend, the governor of Florida. As leaders, when we affirm someone face-to-face we can have an enormous impact on them.

"T" Is For Timely

My mother used to say, "Don't wait until I'm in the grave to say a bunch of nice things about me." We must be quick to affirm and encourage others. The longer we wait the more it loses its full impact.

CONSTANTLY CONFER AFFIRMATION

Do you intentionally affirm your people? Do you encourage your troops often? These days, I believe there's a tremendous hunger for encouragement amongst people in the workplace. The founder of Chick-Fil-A, S. Truett Cathy once said, "How do you know if a man needs encouragement? If he is breathing." Are your people breathing? If so, you should be encouraging them. Many great entrepreneurs built their empires by encouraging others. I read in several publications how Sam Walton, the founder of Wal-Mart went out of his way to encourage his workers. Walton believed it was paramount that everyone that came into his store feel welcomed. Concerning this matter Sam Walton said, "Nothing else can quite substitute for a few well chosen, well-timed, sincere words of praise. They're absolutely free and worth a fortune." Estimate how much it costs you to give someone a compliment. A kind word doesn't cost a penny but it's priceless.

EMOTIONAL BANK ACCOUNTS

I want to radically change the way you view people. Imagine that everyone you come in contact with has an emotional account. When you serve or affirm someone you are making deposits into their emotional account. When you ignore, scream, command, or snap at someone you immediately make a withdrawal. Are you aware of the emotional bank balances of the people you lead? Do you make more deposits than you make withdrawals? In life, problems and conflicts occur when we start to withdraw more than we are depositing. Many problems in our personal and professional lives stem from insufficient funds in our emotional accounts. Today and for the rest of your life commit to making more deposits than withdrawals.

REWARDED BEHAVIOR IS REPEATED BEHAVIOR

Recognition reaps results. Recognition comes in several forms; it may be given to individuals or to groups of people. It may be as simple as "Wow! You did a great job!" Whatever the method, reward your people openly and frequently. Come up with excuses to throw a celebration. The best way to perpetuate progress

> *The best way to perpetuate progress is to reward it and celebrate openly.*

is to reward it and celebrate openly. Never hoard the credit. Spread it out evenly. Always give credit where credit is due. Strive to create a climate where people can get involved and feel important. Discover ways to increase other people's ability to feel as though they are making a significant contribution to your organization. Former U.S. President, Harry S. Truman once said, "You can accomplish anything in life, provided that you do not mind who gets the credit." Don't worry about who gets the credit. Don't just think nice things, say them too. "Good thoughts not delivered means squat," says Ken Blanchard. People accomplish Herculean feats when they are recognized and encouraged. Dan T. Cathy, President and COO of Chick-fil-A put it this way, "People repeat behavior that's recognized and rewarded."

GIVE PRAISE OFTEN, REPRIMAND SPARINGLY

Transformative leaders look through a window when they want to compliment and into a mirror when they want to criticize. American scholar, author, and editor William Arthur Ward once said, "Flatter me, and I may not believe you. Criticize me, and I may not like you. Ignore me, and I may not forgive you. Encourage me, and I will not forget you. Love me and I may be forced to love you." There's always something positive you can affirm, look for it!

PICK THEM UP WHEN THEY FALL

Leaders empower others by having them do more. When you allow those you lead to take on more risks they will inevitably make mistakes. It's part of the journey. When they fall you should be the first to pick them up. When a leader gives a word of encouragement when a teammate fails it is worth more than an hour of praise after success.

GO BENEATH THE SURFACE

Once upon a time, a man was exploring the insides of several caves by the seashore. In one of the caves he found bags with several hardened pieces of clay. It seemed like someone had rolled up some bags of clay and left them in this mysterious bag.

So the man took the bag of hardened clay and began to throw them into the ocean. One by one he threw them until one of them fell on the floor and cracked. What the man saw inside the clay was astounding. In these hardened pieces of clay were expensive rubies. He was shocked!

The man was so excited that he began to break the pieces of clay and found thousand of dollars worth of rubies. His biggest regret is that he could have had thousands of dollars more, had he not thrown the rubies into the ocean. The same is true with people, they may look hard on the outside but they have treasure on the inside of them. Leaders invest

> *Leaders invest the time to draw out the treasures in people.*

the time to draw out the treasures in people. With certain people you have to dig deeper but it's there. Leaders make the big investments and reap the dividends.

BE A DAY MAKER NOT A DAY BREAKER

Hairdresser and entrepreneur, David Wagner, believes in making his clients' day. When one of his regulars called him one morning and said she needed to come in because she had an important appointment that night, Wagner gladly scheduled her in. They laughed, talked, caught up, and had a terrific time. Afterwards he told her how stunning she looked and sent her on way to her "urgent" appointment. She thanked him profusely.

You can imagine David's shock and surprise when he received a handwritten letter from the woman explaining that the important event she wanted to look good for that evening was her own funeral. She had staged her suicide that evening. After she left David's store and felt the abundance of love and care she decided not to kill herself.

This woman's story marked a turning point for David. He realized that his purpose was far greater than simply cutting and styling hair. This prompted David to change his job title to "Daymaker." Today, David and his team strive to make the day of every single person that comes into his salon. David is the owner of ten successful spas that serve dozens of people each day. David even trains his people with the doctrine of "daymakers." Great leaders are great "daymakers." What if you strived to make the day of everyone who worked for you? What if you purposed to exceed their expectations? When you lift up others you lift your leadership to the next level. Children's activist and founder of the Children's Defense Fund, Marian Wright Edelman put it his way, "We must not, in trying to think about how we can make a big difference, ignore the small daily differences we can make which, over time, add up to big differences that we often cannot foresee."

> **When you lift up others you lift your leadership to the next level.**

STUDY GUIDE SECTION

KEY POINTS

While reading, What principles on Affirming Your Team stood out to you the most? Why?

_____

_____

_____

REAL LIFE APPLICATION: PUTTING THE PRINCIPLES AND LESSONS INTO ACTION!

How will you apply this new information to your personal life?

_____

_____

_____

What are some obstacles that get in the way of giving your teammates affirmation? What are some practical steps you can take to help remove some of those obstacles?

_____

_____

_____

PRACTICAL APPLICATION EXERCISE

Step 1- Identify a teammate at work that is doing a fantastic job.

Step 2- Write him or her a handwritten letter expressing your gratitude.

Step 3- Send them the letter.

_____

_____

_____

RATE YOURSELF

Overall, how well and how often do you give your teammates affirmation?

(Check One Box Below)

Poor	Below Average	Average	Satisfactory	Excellent
1	2	3	4	5
☐	☐	☐	☐	☐

I am strongly committed to becoming a CEO or chief encouragement officer for my organization. In other words, I commit to living a lifestyle of encouraging my teammates on a regular basis.

(Check One Box Below)

Poor	Below Average	Average	Satisfactory	Excellent
1	2	3	4	5
☐	☐	☐	☐	☐

GROWING GOAL

Write down at least one goal/objective you have for improving the way you affirm your team:

_____

_____

_____

Stepping stone # 1

_____

_____

_____

Stepping stone # 2

_____

_____

_____

JOURNAL ENTRY

Why is giving affirmation so important to leadership?

_____

_____

_____

> "How do you influence others? Emphatically, the best way to influence others is by serving them!"
> — Gibson Sylvestre

> "The measure of a leader is not the number of people who serve the leader, but the number of people served by the leader."
> — Arnold Glasgow, American humorist

5
LEADERS SERVE OTHERS

Great leaders serve others. Great leaders add value to their colleagues, their organizations, and their team. The very definition of the word leader is defined by service. Service and leadership are inseparable. Servant leaders prepare themselves in order to be available to serve the needs of their people.

HOW DOES ONE GAIN INFLUENCE?

Some so called leaders force themselves onto others to in order to gain influence. Some wave their titles around as if it were a magic wand. In reality, leadership is a gift given by followers. Because followers give us the privilege to lead and serve them, they reserve the right to take it back. Emphatically, the best way to influence others is by serving them. Many leaders make it all about them. They forget who helped them get to their current position. We must never forget who helped us achieve what we have achieved. As Charlie Brown once said, "Few people are successful unless other people want them to be." Teams of hard working people are what make companies and communities great, not individuals.

BECOME A SERVANT LEADER

A servant-leader focuses on serving others rather than serving one's self. They are open, transparent, and invite candid feedback from others. A servant-leader takes great pleasure in seeing others reach their full God-given potential. The phrase "servant leadership" was coined by Robert K. Greenleaf in The Servant as Leader, an essay that was published in 1970. In that essay, Greenleaf declared, "The servant-leader is servant first... It begins with the natural feeling that one wants to serve..." They are passionate about serving others. They subscribe to the philosophy that the primary role of leaders is to serve the people, not to be served. American humorist Arnold Glasgow says, "The measure of a leader is not the number of people who serve the leader, but the number of people served by the leader." Great leaders do not believe that greatness is found in a position. Civil Rights leader Dr. Martin Luther King, Jr. put it this way, "Greatness is determined by service." Many people desire leadership positions because they want to be served. Servant leaders view their positions as a vehicle to serve as many people as possible. Service and leadership are indispensable from each other. Leadership expert Steven Covey once said, "The servant leader is one who seeks to draw out, inspire, and develop the best and

> *Service and leadership are indispensable from each other.*

highest within people from the inside out." Servant leaders are always asking, "How can I make this situation better? How can I serve better? Who needs help right now?" Author William Ward once summarizes leadership like this, "We must be silent before we can listen. We must listen before we can learn. We must learn before we can prepare. We must prepare before we can serve. We must serve before we can lead." In other words, the quintessential prerequisite for leadership is serving others.

LEAD BY CHOOSING SUPER SERVICE OVER SELF-SERVICE

Again, whoever thinks leadership is putting your feet on top of a desk and ordering people around is sadly mistaken. Success coach Brian Tracy says, "Successful people are always looking for opportunities to help others. Unsuccessful people are always asking, "What's in it for me?" In order to be a "super service leader" here are some principles that will help you:

1. Lead From The Front

Leading from the front is about taking risks for your team. A great example of this is Julius Caesar. Caesar was one of the most celebrated Roman political and military leaders. In Caesar's days most kings would lead from the back. They would send their troops up front and watch them fight. The frontline was the most dangerous location of the battlefield. Caesar was different because Caesar led from the front. When his men saw him taking this enormous risk they fought even harder. Are you willing to lead from the front?

2. Sacrifice For Your Team

Great leaders are defined by the sacrifices they make for others. Martin Luther King, Jr. sacrificed his life to fight for minority rights in the United States. Mother Teresa sacrificed a comfortable life with her wealthy family to help the poor and downtrodden in Calcutta, India. American novelist and poet John Updike once said, "A leader is one who, out of madness or goodness, volunteers to take on himself the woe of the people. There are few men so foolish, hence the erratic quality of leadership." Most people don't want to sacrifice their comforts and convenience for others.

A great example of a sacrificial leader is Alexander The Great. Alexander conquered the entire known world by the time he was thirty years old. How did someone so young accomplish such a colossal feat? How did this seemingly young man command so much respect and loyalty? I personally believe that Alexander The Great was an effective leader because he served others. One time his men had been fighting for weeks in the desert. Most of them were chronically dehydrated. It was a gloomy time for Alexander and his troops. Some of the men where near death due to dehydration. In the midst of their peril one of the men found a small container of water. He quickly ran to Alexander and said, "Quickly drink this, you look like you're about pass out!" Everyone on his team stared at that cup of water as though it was worth all the riches of the world. Alexander poured the cup of water on the ground and yelled, "It is no use to drink when so many thirst!" Alexander gained the respect of his men by sacrificing for them. I find it interesting to note, he is not referred to by his real name, which is, "Alexandros III Philppou Makedonon." He is referred to as, "Alexander The Great." Why the title great? I believe people called him great because he was a sacrificial servant leader.

3. Become A Level Five Leader!

What is a level five leader? How is a level five leader defined? Jim Collins, author of Good To Great says, "Level 5 leaders channel their ego needs away from themselves and into the larger goal of building a great company. It's not that Level 5 leaders have no ego or self-interest. Indeed, they are incredibly ambitious – but their ambition is first and foremost for the institution, not themselves." In other words, level five leaders look out for the best interest of their organizations. They go beyond the call of duty. Are you a level five leader? If not, how can you position yourself to become a level five leader?

MAKE THEM FEEL SPECIAL

In my book, Staying Positive In A Negative World, I stress the importance of treating people like gold. I say, "Treat your people like gold because they are!" Transformational leaders specialize in making others feel good about themselves. Author J. Carla Nortcutt put it this way, "The goal of

Treat your people like gold because they are!

many leaders is to get people to think more highly of the leader. The goal of a great leader is to help people to think more highly of themselves." Imagine everyone you ever meet having a sign saying, "M.M.F.S.P." The acronym stands for: MAKE ME FEEL SPECIAL PLEASE! It's the cry of every heart. Everyone deserves "MAKE ME FEEL SPECIAL PLEASE" treatment, even those that act mean, pessimistic, and negative. James Kouzes and Barry Posner in their landmark leadership book entitled, *Credibility*, put it this way, "Leaders we admire do not place themselves at the center; they place others there. They do not seek the attention of people; they give it to others. They do not focus on satisfying their own aims and desires; they look for ways to respond to the needs and interests of their constituents. They are not self-centered; they concentrate on the constituent... Leaders serve a purpose and the people who have made it possible for them to lead..." We admire leaders who make us feel we can conquer the world. They empower us. They inspire us. They invigorate us!

DO SMALL THINGS WITH GREAT LOVE

Transformational leaders do small things well. As Mother Teresa once said, "We can do no great things, only small things with great love." That's exactly what great leaders do; they know that big things are simply a compilation of many small things. Nothing is ever beneath a true transformational leader. As bestselling author Max Lucado says, "Don't be too big to do something too small."

LEADING IS GIVING

Essentially, serving others is about giving of ourselves. It requires a significant amount of energy to fully give of ourselves. Leadership expert Mark Sanborn once said, "When you make the world better for others, you make the world better for yourself. For the 20-odd years I've worked in leadership development, I've observed that giving – being of service – can be the most overlooked aspect of leadership, whatever your title. Usually, when we think of leadership we think of performance, effectiveness and results. But those critical aspects of leadership shine all the more brightly when they coexist with giving, service and contribution." What is your contribution going to be? What impact will you make on others? Making a difference doesn't have to be very dramatic. World renowned professional tennis player Arthur Ashe once said, "True heroism is remarkably sober, very undramatic. It is not the urge to surpass all others at whatever cost,

> **Making a difference doesn't have to be very dramatic.**

but the urge to serve others at whatever the cost." Most of the time the greatest things that we can do are the small things that no one puts on the front page.

SERVING OTHERS BENEFITS THE COMPANY AS A WHOLE

The people who serve the most add the most value to others. The greater your contribution the more your company prospers. Leadership guru Tom Peters once said, "The best kept secret in the global economy today is this: When your service is AWESOME you get so stinking rich you have to buy new bags to carry all the money home." The purpose of serving is certainly not monetary rewards. However, the most successful and wealthy people on the planet are those that serve the most. For example, Sam Walton, the founder of Wal-Mart is in the top one percent of the wealthiest people in the world. In Walton's biography his main goal for starting Wal-Mart was to serve the middle class of America with the lowest priced retail items ever. Sam Walton has passed on into eternity, yet his heirs are still amongst the worlds richest.

BE SENSITIVE TO THE NEEDS OF OTHERS

Leaders are sensitive to the needs of others. They genuinely care about the people they are leading. Learning people skills are important for anyone contemplating a career in leadership. Do not just hear what people say with their mouths, hear their hearts. Love people. Always bless the people around you. Always ask yourself, "How can I serve someone today? How can I exceed someone's expectations today? How can I make someone's day?" Great leaders are empathetic towards others. They constantly walk in the shoes of others. Empathetic leaders earn the loyalty of their followers. Are you compassionate about those you lead? Do you show them you care? Is it demonstrated by your actions?

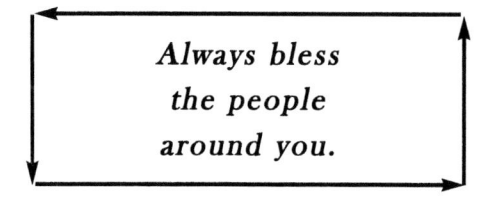

Always bless the people around you.

HERB KELLEHER: SERVING BY EXAMPLE

Herb Kelleher is one of the most celebrated CEOs in United States history. Kelleher founded Southwest Airlines.

He embodies what it means to be a servant leader. Concerning servant leadership Kelleher says, "I'd describe leadership as servant hood. ... The best leaders have to be good followers as well. You have to be willing to subject your own ego to the needs of your business." When leaders serve, everyone around them gets energized. When leaders serve, they bring out the best in others. There is no ego in serving others. James Kouzes and Barry Posner in their landmark leadership book entitled, *Credibility*, point out, "In serving a purpose, leaders strengthen credibility by demonstrating that they are not in it for themselves; instead, they have the interests of the institution, department, or team and its constituents at heart. Being a servant may not be what many leaders had in mind when they choose to take responsibility for the vision and direction of their organization or team, but serving others is the most glorious and rewarding of all leadership tasks." When we serve others we are more blessed than the people we serve. When people realize that we are not in it for ourselves, mistrust disappears and a high level of trust increases. Kelleher's mission was to literally "serve the servers." Kelleher would help with the baggage. He would hand out peanuts. Periodically, he would even serve as a flight attendant; that is unheard of for most high-powered CEOs today. Most leaders today are so puffed up that they are self-deceived. These types of leaders are like toxic waste to the companies that employ them. Self serving leaders destroy companies. Leadership powerhouse Ken Blanchard put it this way, "When people leave companies, they tend not to quit the company; they are more likely to have quit the boss." Because of Kelleher's electrifying, fun-loving, servant leadership people lined up to work for his company. For instance, in 1996, Southwest received 124,000 applications for 5,444 job openings. Wow! Amazing huh? Even today, Southwest Airlines enjoys international renown for being a great place to work, because everyone wants to work for a leader who serves them. Sheila Murray Bethel author of *Making a Difference: 12 Qualities That Make You a Leader* says, "If leadership serves only the leader, it will fail. Ego satisfaction, financial gain, and status can all be valuable tools for a leader, but if they become the only motivations, they will eventually destroy a leader. Only when service for a common good is the primary purpose, are you truly leading." Lead with other people's best interest in mind. If you look out for others they will look out for you. As motivational legend Zig Ziglar says, "You can only get what you want, if you help enough other people get what they want."

> **If you look out for others they will look out for you.**

STUDY GUIDE SECTION

KEY POINTS

While reading, What principles of Servant leadership stood out to you the most? Why?

_____

_____

_____

REAL LIFE APPLICATION: PUTTING THE PRINCIPLES AND LESSONS INTO ACTION!

How will you apply this new information to your personal life?

_____

_____

_____

What are some obstacles that get in the way of you having a servant's heart towards your teammates? What are some practical steps you can take to help remove some of those obstacles?

_____

_____

_____

PRACTICAL APPLICATION EXERCISE

Step 1- Plan a picnic for your staff.

Step 2- Have your leadership staff serve the rest of your team. (This includes set up and clean up as well.)

_____

_____

_____

RATE YOURSELF

Overall, how well do you display a servant's heart towards your team?

(Check One Box Below)

Poor	Below Average	Average	Satisfactory	Excellent
1	2	3	4	5
☐	☐	☐	☐	☐

I am strongly committed to becoming a servant leader.

(Check One Box Below)

Poor	Below Average	Average	Satisfactory	Excellent
1	2	3	4	5
☐	☐	☐	☐	☐

GROWING GOAL

Write down at least one goal/objective you have for becoming a servant leader:

_____

_____

Stepping stone # 1

_____

_____

_____

Stepping stone # 2

_____

_____

_____

Stepping stone # 3

_____

_____

_____

JOURNAL ENTRY

Write down ten ways you can serve your teammates on a regular basis.

_____

_____

_____

_____

> "Leaders are liberators, lawgivers try to lockdown."
> — Gibson Sylvestre

> "If you want to go fast, go alone. If you want to go far, go together."
> — Patty Stonesifer, Former co-chair and chief executive officer of the Bill and Melinda Gates Foundation

6
SHARE THE LEADERSHIP

The best leaders in the world share their leadership. No man is an island. A leader will never reach his or her full potential alone. It's been said that it's lonely at the top. I have often wondered, does leadership really have to be so lonely? The answer is no. Leaders make it lonely by being too reclusive. Furthermore, leaders make it lonely by hoarding the power. Transformational leaders share the power with others. Former co-chair and chief executive officer of the Bill and Melinda Gates Foundation Patty Stonesifer, once said, "If you want to go fast, go alone. If you want to go far, go together." When you "go together" life is tremendously more joyful. Developing and motivating employees is not one-size-fits-all. Know what motivates your people. Know your people. In today's burgeoning world, leaders must commit themselves to multiplying leadership in every corner of their organizations. Former first lady Eleanor Roosevelt put it this way, "Perhaps in His wisdom the Almighty is trying to show us that a leader may chart the way... but that many leaders and many peoples must do the building." Share the leadership and watch your organization skyrocket.

FOUR FEARS LEADERS HAVE OF EMPOWERING OTHERS TO LEAD

Many leaders fear sharing their power. They believe it will work against them. However, sharing the power is where you see true transformation. Even if you have been hurt in the past, I am asking you to forgive and trust again. Learn from those that hurt you. Don't make the same mistakes. Proceed forward with caution.

Remember, fear stands for:
False
Evidence
Appearing
Real

Here are some of the main reasons leaders are afraid of empowering others:

1. I won't be needed anymore. Many leaders believe if they empower others they won't be needed anymore. The opposite is true. When you empower others you will be needed more. Let me explain. When the fire of empowerment is released throughout your organization, your role will need to shift from manager to coach. You will be inundated with an overabundance of opportunities to coach your rising stars.

2. I won't have as much authority anymore. In actuality, you will have more authority. People will come to respect and admire your humility. It's only when you seek authority that you ironically lose it.

3. The work won't get done as good as I would do it. At first, people will either sink or soar. You have to prepare yourself to be okay with allowing some of your people to fail. If they turn in faulty work, return it back to

> *...be okay with allowing some of your people to fail.*

them in love and say, "I believe in you. I know you are more than capable of doing better work than this."

4. Fear the staff member is not prepared. News Flash: Your staff will never be prepared. Push them out of the frying pan and into the fire. Remember you can never learn how to ride a bike by reading about it. At some point you have to get on the bike and start practicing. Yes, there will be some mistakes but the benefits outweigh the detriments. World renowned clergyman D.L. Moody once said, "I'd rather get ten men to do the job than do the job of ten men.

ENABLE OTHERS TO SUCCEED

Great leaders enable others to succeed. They remove barriers that stand in the way of people and their success. Here are some ways that leaders can help people succeed and reach their highest potential.

1. Truly care for your people. When you are for your people it changes everything about the way you relate to them. When you demonstrate that you care they have an even greater desire to succeed and not let you down.

2. Be fully present when interacting with them. When you pay full attention to the group you are leading they perceive that you feel they are important and they will perform to their highest potential.

3. Seek out opportunities to serve them. A serving leader is a superb leader.

4. Make decisions and take actions with your followers' needs in mind. When you make decisions in your own interest you shortcut the success of your people. Always think of your constituents when making decisions.

5. Provide assignments that challenge your folks to grow and develop. Don't be afraid to challenge your team. They want to be challenged. If you don't challenge them they will get bored.

6. Acknowledge and reward strengths and progress made by your team. People love to get recognition. Use rewards to appreciate excellent work as well promote excellent work.

7. Accept some risk (and even failure) as a part of the master plan. Businessman Timothy Firnstahl once said, "Delegating means letting others become the experts and hence the best." We become experts through making and correcting our mistakes. When your people make mistakes use it as a teaching moment. Don't shy away from failure. Some of the best discoveries in life came about because of failure. In the book, *The Leadership Challenge*, authors Kouzes and Posner write, "True leaders foster risk taking, encouraging others to step out into the unknown, rather than play it safe." Teach your people to attempt great feats.

> Some of the best discoveries in life came about because of failure.

TOP-DOWN LEADERSHIP IS OUT TO STAY

Top-down leadership is outdated and antiquated. We are in a new era of leadership. Motivational speaker and author Suzanne Zoglio once said, "As leaders shift their focus to customers and quality, they realize that the old authoritarian leadership style does not work anymore. To achieve quality, service, and rapid response, leaders must utilize all available talent. They must find ways to inspire, involve, and empower employees. They must create a work environment that encourages commitment, innovation, and cooperation. Instead of evaluating, leaders now coach. Instead of doing, they delegate. Instead of telling, they facilitate. No one is expected to boss anyone. Everyone is expected to participate." The world has changed, never to return to the old. The top-down leadership model was engineered for the Industrial Age. Top-down leadership was used to control factory workers viewed as nothing more than extensions of machines. Dehumanizing huh? Controlling doesn't work anymore. As they say, "Over managing is one of the cardinal sins of leadership." Today, we are in the Information Age where workers have a lot more leverage and access to knowledge. The founding of the United States of America was based on the premise that government exists to serve the people, not that people exist to serve the government. That's not to say that we don't roll up our sleeves and help our government. As John F. Kennedy said, "Don't ask what your country can do for you; rather ask what you can do for your country." The Pilgrims left Britain because of its government paradigm. In England, the people were subjects serving the Crown. In America everyone was free to elect who they wanted to govern them and even reject whomever they wanted to reject. In America the power comes from the bottom-up. In England, the power came from the top-down. My friend, the top-down system of governance died with the Industrial Age. As Ray Smith, CEO of Bell-Atlantic once declared, "To create a high performance team we must replace typical management activities like supervising, checking, monitoring, and controlling with new behaviors like coaching and communicating." The old model is dead. The new model i.e. servant leadership is here to stay.

THE ART OF DELEGATION

As a leader, success is knowing the great art of directing others without them noticing it. In other words, delegating should be effortless. Delegating is more of an art than a science. Here are some insightful principles of delegating:

1. Delegation Multiplies The Leader's Time

If a leader is constantly complaining that he doesn't have enough time, that's a sure indicator he's not delegating properly. Wise leaders delegate tasks in proportion to their staff member's follow-through track record.

2. Delegation Teaches The Leader Self-Control

At first, it will be difficult for you not to micromanage. However, delegating is a surefire way to teaching you the art of self-control. United States President Theodore Roosevelt put it this way, "The best executive is the one who has sense enough to pick good men to do what he wants done, and self-restraint enough to keep from meddling with them while they do it." When you take back a task that you have delegated you are totally disempowering your staff member. Malcolm S. Forbes, publisher of Forbes Magazine once said, "If you don't know what to do with many of the papers piled on your desk, stick a dozen colleague's initials on them and pass them along. When in doubt, route." And when you route, stay away. Legendary United States Military General, George S. Patton, Jr. put it this way, "Never tell people how to do things. Tell them what to do and they will surprise you with their ingenuity."

> *When you take back a task... you are disempowering your staff member.*

3. Delegation Leverages The Leader's Intellect

Astute leaders leverage their intellect. They are inquisitive learners. They are always asking questions. I recently read that Bill Gates, Founder and CEO of Microsoft is a ferocious learner. Gates once said that the reason he and his team study so much is because he believes Microsoft is always in a state of being, "two years from being obsolete." Wow! I can't think of many companies that come close to Microsoft's innovation but Bill Gates believes he always needs to be striving to be on the cutting edge. One time Bill Gates found out that one of his staff members knew more about a particular technology than he did, so he sat with this individual for weeks until he was up to par. Some might interpret that as being excessively competitive. At any rate, like Bill Gates, we as leaders must borrow from the intellect of others. As United States President Woodrow

Wilson poignantly said, "I not only use all the brains I have, but all that I can borrow."

4. Delegation Serves As An Example To Your Team

The speed of the leader is usually the speed of the team. When we don't work with diligence our team follows our example. A friend of mine once said, "The leader's floor is his follower's ceiling." Wow! That simply means we need to drastically increase our floor. Leadership consultant Robert Half once said, "Delegating work works, provided the one delegating works, too." In other words, delegation is not some highfalutin substitute for being lazy. Leaders must lead by example.

THE TRANSCENDENCE OF EMPOWERMENT

Inside everyone you lead there's magic. Leaders know how to draw the magic out. Author Blaine Lee once quipped, "The great leaders are like the best conductors – they reach beyond the notes to reach the magic in the players." Find the beautiful magic in your people. When you find it let them soar!

LEADERS WHO EMPOWER OTHERS LEVERAGE THEIR TEAM'S EFFECTIVENESS

No leader succeeds if his followers don't want him to succeed. Think about that statement. The power and influence you enjoy was given to you by those who follow you. That reality brings humility to the whole business of leadership. Business mogul Monte L. Bean once said, "If there is any one axiom that I have tried to live up to in trying to become successful in business, it is the fact that I have tried to surround myself with associates that know more about business than I do.

This policy has always been very successful and is still working for me." Surround yourself with great people and you shall become great. But never forget who got you to the top. Never become egotistical. The minute you get egotistical, the same people that help you get to the top will fight to bring you down. "An empowered organization is one in which individuals have the knowledge, skill, desire, and opportunity to personally succeed in a way that leads to collective organizational success," says Stephen Covey. Servant leaders strive for collective success, not personal success.

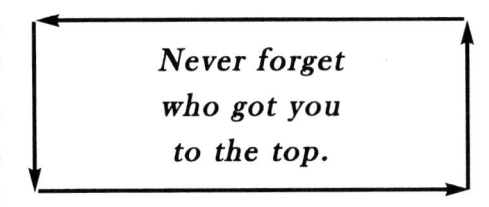

> ***Never forget who got you to the top.***

ARE YOU A LEADER OR A LID, A LIBERATOR OR A LAWGIVER?

Parents love to see their children do better in life than they have done. In the same way, transformational leaders like to see those that they have led do better than they have done; that is the essence of leadership. A lid leader is what I call a "crab" leader. If you want to keep crabs in a bucket you put other crabs in there with him. As soon as one crab tries to get out the other crabs pull him back in. This is exactly what lid leaders do. If they see someone under their leadership who has greater gifts they viciously try to sabotage them. But great leaders want their people to be their very best. Here is the difference between leaders and lids, liberators and lawgivers:

1. Leaders are liberators, lawgivers try to lockdown.
Any leader worth his salt makes his team better not worse.

When they see someone starting to take flight they become the wind beneath their wings. Former Secretary of Defense Donald Rumsfeld once declared, "Don't be a bottleneck. If a matter is not a decision for the President or you, delegate it. Force responsibility down and out. Find problem areas, add structure and delegate. The pressure is to do the reverse. Resist it."
Leaders must let up to help others get up!

2. Leaders lead and don't get involved in micromanaging, lids love to micromanage. Leaders show up and shut up. Hey don't control the patrol. Former U.S. President Ronald Reagan put it this way, "Surround yourself with the best people you can find, delegate authority, and don't interfere."

3. Leaders share the credit, lids steal the credit.
Small leaders love to steal the credit. In our organization, if something goes wrong I blame myself, if something goes right I blame my team. Industrialist Andrew Carnegie observed, "No person will make a great business who wants to do it all himself or get all the credit." Transformative leaders share the credit. No one likes to work their hardest and have the credit stolen.

THE LAWS OF EMPOWERMENT

As leaders, we are all called to empower others. Empowering others is a journey. Many people doubt themselves. They lack the confidence to accomplish their goals. Leaders help others

Leaders help others increase their confidence.

increase their confidence. Here are some powerful principles that will help you successfully empower your team:

Law # 1- Leave Out The Eggs

Empower those who work with you by giving them significant projects to complete. Deep inside the human heart, man wants to contribute something of great value. Many cake mixes leave out the eggs. Have you ever stopped and asked why? They leave out the eggs because when you and I crack those eggs and mix the ingredients together we feel like we are accomplishing something big, even if it was minor. How can you leave out the eggs for the people in your company? Remember, leaders leave out the eggs. Microsoft Founder and CEO Bill Gates once said, "As we look ahead into the next century, leaders will be those who empower others." Show your team that you need them. One of the most basic human needs is the need to be needed. Harvey S. Firestone, Founder of the Firestone Tire and Rubber Company, once said, "The growth and development of people is the highest calling of leadership." Your people are your greatest asset.

Law # 2- Empowerment Enhances Team Performance

Empowering others multiplies your team's impact. Drastic changes in performance occur more quickly when your teammates get in the game. Growth comes from being in the game, not the stands. When you start empowering others your performance improves.

Law # 3- Empowerment Fosters Loyalty

Once you develop the reputation as being a "people builder" people will flock to your doors. Your staff becomes incredibly loyal to your cause when you empower them.

Law # 4- Empowerment Opens The Door To Learning

When people feel empowered they want to learn all the more. The more they know the more they become valuable to the organization.

Law # 5- Empowerment Prepares Your Organization For Succession Planning

Many corporate leaders and managers are ambitious about climbing the corporate ladder. Every good leader prepares those who follow him to take his place. There's no such thing as success without a successor. Jack Welch of General Electric had a knack for developing leaders. Every two weeks he would fly in a private helicopter to Crotonville, New York to help train budding leaders. As busy as he was, he took leadership development extremely serious. In fact, he didn't miss a single session for sixteen years. That's commitment.

THE PRACTICAL PRACTICES OF GREAT COACHES

Step 1- Tell them what to do. Be specific, let them know exactly what you want to accomplish.

Step 2- Show them how to do it. Demonstrate how it's done. However, don't tie them down to doing it your way. They may actually know a more efficient way of doing it.

Step 3- Let them show you how to do it. Have them show you, so that you can coach them and help build their confidence.

Step 4- Let them tell what they just did. Get feedback. Feedback is critical to your teammate's success.

Step5- Tell them how they did. Give them your constructive criticism. Show them how they can improve, but emphasize what they did correctly.

Step 6- Celebrate small gains and successes. Periodically celebrate incremental gains and progress. Make celebration a standard part of your corporate culture.

YOUR PEOPLE ALREADY HAVE IT

Your people already have leadership inside of them. Think about it, an art student doesn't go to art school to get the gift of being an artist. He or she goes to art school to sharpen the gift that's already inside of them. Many of your troops have gems on the inside of them. Dig them up. Encourage them. Build them up. Call them higher. Don't hold them back. Let them soar!

> *Many of your troops have gems on the inside of them. Dig them up.*

STUDY GUIDE SECTION

KEY POINTS

While reading, What principles on sharing the leadership stood out to you the most? Why?

_____

_____

_____

REAL LIFE APPLICATION: PUTTING THE PRINCIPLES AND LESSONS INTO ACTION!

How will you apply this new information to your personal life?

_____

_____

_____

What are some obstacles that get in the way of you giving more leadership responsibilities to your team members? What are some practical steps you can take to help remove some of those obstacles?

_____

_____

_____

PRACTICAL APPLICATION EXERCISE

Step 1- Identify a teammate that has leadership potential.

Step 2- Delegate one aspect of your job to that person.

Step 3- Be available to answer questions and serve as a coach.

_____

_____

_____

RATE YOURSELF

Overall, how well and how often do you give leadership opportunities to others?

(Check One Box Below)

Poor	Below Average	Average	Satisfactory	Excellent
1	2	3	4	5
❏	❏	❏	❏	❏

I am strongly committed to becoming a better team player.

(Check One Box Below)

Poor	Below Average	Average	Satisfactory	Excellent
1	2	3	4	5
❏	❏	❏	❏	❏

GROWING GOAL

Write down at least one goal/objective you have for becoming better at sharing your leadership with others:

_____

_____

_____

Stepping stone # 1

_____

_____

_____

Stepping stone # 2

_____

_____

_____

Stepping stone # 3

_____

_____

_____

JOURNAL ENTRY
Why is sharing leadership so important?

> "Success is the easy part, sustainability is what's difficult. Is your success as a leader sustainable? Is your pace sustainable? The way you handle stress and manage your energy will determine your longevity."
> — Gibson Sylvestre

> "Give to yourself until your cup runneth over then give to others out of your overflow."
> — Anonymous

7
LEADERS KNOW WHEN TO RECHARGE THEIR BATTERIES

Transformational leaders have a fire in their stomach about their work. They love what they do. They love it so much that their biggest temptation is spend too much time working on "the dream." This chapter is about learning to lead a balanced life. Success is the easy part, sustainability is what's difficult. Is your success as a leader sustainable? Is your pace sustainable? The way you handle stress and manage your energy will determine your longevity.

ARE YOU A FADING FIRECRACKER OR CONSTANT CONSTELLATION?

Leaders come in two forms. They are either "fading firecrackers" or "constant constellations." The "fading firecrackers" are the loud boisterous ones. Everyone who looks at them sees their immense potential. However, like firecrackers they make a lot of noise, put on a good show, and in the end they just fade into oblivion. They are like those rock-n-roll bands that burst onto the scene with one hit and you never hear about them ever again. They are your "one hit wonders." On the other hand, the "constant constellations" lead steady and sustainable lives. You maybe wondering, what is their secret? Their secret is they have taken the time on the front end to plan and prepare their strategy for long-term success. In other words, they have a predetermined pace that will enable them to lead their organizations while having a healthy home life, a healthy body, and a healthy professional life. Now ask yourself, which one do you want to be, a "fading firecracker" or a "constant constellation?"

STRESS: ALL LEADERS ARE VULNERABLE TO IT

Every leader is vulnerable to being overtaken by stress. The barrenness of business can be daunting. The Ideas2Action Study in conjunction with the Center for Creative Leadership found that:

- Eighty-eight percent of leaders report that work is their primary source of stress in their lives and that having a leadership role increases the level of stress they experience.
- More than 60 percent of those leaders surveyed say that their organizations failed to provide them with the tools necessary to manage stress.

These statistics are alarming. First, they tell us that the majority of leaders are in danger of leadership burnout. Second, they tell us that many organizations are not helping leaders manage the plethora of stressors associated with leadership. This reinforces the fact that leaders must take responsibility upon themselves to help manage the stress in their lives. No one will take better care of you than you will, because nobody knows you better than you know yourself.

WHAT IS LEADERSHIP BURNOUT?

Many people ask me, what is burnout? Leadership burnout is a physical, mental and emotional response to constant levels of high stress, lack of exercise, and lack of balance in a leader's life. Leadership burnout often arises from unrealistic demands on a leader's schedule, combined with workaholic habits left unchecked. These pressures are sometimes internal (high expectations of ourselves, emotional exhaustion) or external (marriage issues, wayward teenagers, family trauma, work changes, etc.).

> *Leadership burnout often arises from unrealistic demands on a leader's schedule...*

MAJOR CAUSES OF LEADERSHIP BURNOUT

Reason # 1- Poor time management practices. When leaders don't manage time properly, they run the risk of getting burnt out. Time is a nonrenewable asset, use it as such. If you protect your time, it will protect you against leadership burnout.

Reason # 2- Not prioritizing key relationships in your life. Relationships matter! When you let pursuing your goals get in the way of key relationships you have gone too far.

Reason # 3- Unrealistic expectations of ourselves. No man or woman is a superhero. We can only do so much. If you overextend yourself, you will pay a hefty price for it. It's good to push ourselves, but be realistic! Only do what you can.

Reason # 4- Not supplying yourself with basic human needs. We are not robots; we need sleep, food, rest, leisure, and etc.

Reason # 5- Not having clear objectives. When leaders don't have clear targets they get frustrated. How do you know when you have reached your goals? If you can't answer that question you are in trouble. Take some time and define what the win looks like for you.

Reason # 6- Insufficient training for your new role. Even if you feel undertrained grow into your new role at a sustainable pace. Don't fall into the trap of doing too much too soon.

Reason # 7- Constantly being overwhelmed. The never ending feeling that there is too much to do is what drives leaders off the deep end. No human being can function properly with an overwhelming sense of inadequateness. At some point we all need to feel that we are making progress. If not, we lose hope and losing hope is very dangerous in the life of a leader.

Reason # 8- Being constantly overworked and in a frenzy. When your life is like this, leadership is no fun. Leadership is not about being overworked and unbalanced. If you are constantly feeling overwhelmed seriously invest some time learning how to delegate. It can literally save your life.

Reason # 9- Conflicts on the job. Resolve conflicts immediately! When you let conflicts sit too long the whole office begins to stink. It's like heating fish in a microwave, after awhile the entire house smells like fish. Resolve conflicts and move on.

Reason # 10- Inability to set boundaries and say "no!" Great leaders learn how to say, "No!" Learning to say, "no" can actually save your sanity.

Reason # 11- Not feeling appreciated on the job. Not feeling appreciated leads to frustration. A perpetual state of frustration leads to leadership burnout.

SYMPTOMS OF LEADERSHIP BURNOUT

The symptoms below are serious. If your find yourself or a fellow leader experiencing any of these symptoms, you need to take special attention. Here are the symptoms of leadership burnout:

1. Constant irritability.
2. Loss of appetite.
3. Insomnia.
4. Depression.
5. Feeling tired all the time.
6. Muscle Tension.
7. Headaches.
8. Lack of effectiveness. Spinning wheels and not getting anywhere.
9. Lack of zest for life.
10. Lack of joy.
11. Anxiety.
12. Over dramatizing small issues.

If you are experiencing any of these symptoms you need to halt. Whenever I teach people who struggle with addictive behavior I give them this acronym called H.A.L.T. which stands for:

Hungry
Angry
Lonely
Tired

Whenever you are hungry, angry, lonely, or tired you are most vulnerable to temptations. In the same regard, whenever you are experiencing the symptoms above, you need to halt all action and seek some help.

IS YOUR CURRENT PACE SUSTAINABLE?

Ask yourself: "Is my current pace sustainable?" If not, please consider making some major changes for the benefit of yourself and family members. Do you have any margin in your schedule? Or is your life scheduled down to the very second? You have the resources it takes to live a happy, well balanced life. All you have to do is plan for it and pay for it. Leadership expert and clergyman Bill Hybels believes that every leader should have a "Planned Negligence Strategy." Hybels means that every leader should have a burnout prevention strategy. This strategy is absolutely necessary for the proliferation of the leader and the organization.

LIFESAVING STRATEGIES TO AVOID LEADERSHIP BURNOUT

1. **Put on your oxygen mask first.** A wise man once said, "Give to yourself until your cup runneth over then give to others out of your overflow." That statement is enormously true. Many times leaders keep giving and giving until they have nothing else to give and eventually they burn out. We proverbially burn the candles at both ends and end up stressing ourselves out. When we get on airplanes the flight attendant always instructs us, in case of an emergency, to put on our mask first before we help others with their masks. If we can't help ourselves, we won't be able to help others. Leadership is about operating in your best interest while operating in the best interest of others at the same time.

2. **Stay positive.** The world has enough negative people.

As leaders we need to be positive role models. I have read numerous studies that prove how staying positive enhances every area in a person's life.

3. Focus on results, not on rushing. Some leaders think, "The busier I am, the better I am." Being busy doesn't mean you are effective. Always ask, "Am I doing what is urgent or important?" Leaders focus on the important things.

4. Take vacations regularly and cut off the office. If you are going to avoid leadership burnout in your life I have three words for you; TAKE A VACATION! I was surprised to learn that many Americans don't take vacations anymore. In fact, the Travel Industry Association of America says:
- In 1997, the average time Americans took off per year was 7.1 days.
- In 2001, it was down to 4.1 days

In addition, the Families & Work Institute reports that,
- One fourth or 25% of all American employees did not EVEN use their vacation time.

Sadly, sometimes leaders get too attached to their work. It seems being a workaholic is celebrated in our society, however, when you get burned out all the celebrating stops. All leaders need time to recharge their batteries. Would you ever attempt to drive across the country without putting gas in your vehicle? Of course not! First of all, you wouldn't get very

> *All leaders need time to recharge their batteries.*

far. And second of all, you would damage your vehicle. Likewise, when we don't take time off to rest we actually damage our bodies and become unproductive. If you are going to win at the game of life and keep stress under control you, must take regular vacations. The word "vacation" comes from the Latin root vacare, which means, "to be unoccupied." When leaders go on vacation they should really, really, "vacate" and totally unplug from their work. British essayist and self-confessed workaholic, G.K. Chesterton, suggested in his essay, "On Leisure," he said that there are three ways to properly enjoy one's leisure:

"The first is being allowed to do something. The second is being allowed to do anything, and the third (and perhaps most rare and precious) is being allowed to do nothing." When you leave for vacation leave these instructions: "Only call me in a dire emergency or if this place is burning down!"

5. Take good care of yourself. Leaders that make it until the end eat healthy foods. They also exercise to relieve stress and get the proper amount of rest.

6. Ask for help. Don't try to do it all yourself. Be humble enough to ask for help. Most people count it a joy to help their leader.

7. Study your symptoms and build boundaries to protect yourself. No one is going to protect you as much as you can protect yourself. Watch out for the symptoms of leadership burnout and be prepared to win against burnout.

8. Stay connected to energizing friends. Meet for brunch, lunch or dinner, at least once a month, with a group of close, fun, and energizing friends. Cut people off who suck the very life out of you. Be around people who energize you.

9. Practice gratitude. Ungratefulness leads to leadership burnout. Ungratefulness leads to envy and strife. However, when we stop to thank our Creator for all His bountiful blessings He's bestowed on us, we begin to experience unbelievable amounts of joy. "Gratitude unlocks the fullness of life. It turns what we have into enough, and more. It turns denial into acceptance, chaos to order, confusion to clarity. It can turn a meal into a feast, a house into a home, a stranger into a friend. Gratitude is all about one word: enough. Gratitude doesn't focus on getting more, it simply acknowledges that whatever one has is already enough. Gratitude makes sense of our past, brings peace for today, and creates a vision for tomorrow," says author Melodie Beattie.

> **When you focus on being grateful, burnout stays far away from you!**

The next time you get stressed take a notebook and begin to count all your blessings. I guarantee you will feel more positive and encouraged! As they say, "He who knows he has enough is rich." Today, write down your accomplishments, triumphs and joy. When you focus on being grateful, burnout stays far away from you!

STUDY GUIDE SECTION

KEY POINTS

While reading, What principles on recharging your batteries stood out to you the most? Why?

_____

_____

_____

REAL LIFE APPLICATION: PUTTING THE PRINCIPLES AND LESSONS INTO ACTION!

How will you apply this new information to your personal life?

_____

_____

_____

What are some obstacles that get in the way of you taking time off? What are some practical steps you can take to help remove some of those obstacles?

_____

_____

_____

PRACTICAL APPLICATION EXERCISE

Step 1- Pick four to five days within the next six months and allocate those days for a vacation.

Step 2- While on vacation, do not bring anything that has to do with work. Make sure your office only calls you in the event of a dire emergency.

Step 3- Enjoy this time with family and friends.

_____

_____

_____

RATE YOURSELF

Overall, how intentional are you when it comes to recharging your batteries?

(Check One Box Below)

Poor	Below Average	Average	Satisfactory	Excellent
1	2	3	4	5
❑	❑	❑	❑	❑

I am strongly committed to having a weekly resting routine.

(Check One Box Below)

Poor	Below Average	Average	Satisfactory	Excellent
1	2	3	4	5
❑	❑	❑	❑	❑

GROWING GOAL

Write down at least one goal/objective you have for Developing a calculated plan that will guarantee you resting and exercising at least one full day per week:

_____

_____

_____

Stepping stone # 1

_____

_____

_____

Stepping stone # 2

_____

_____

_____

Stepping stone # 3

_____

_____

_____

JOURNAL ENTRY

Why is rest so important in the life of a leader? What boundaries have you set up to prevent burnout?

_____

_____

_____

_____

_____

> "Great leaders are defined by the difficult decisions they make. Leadership is all about having the courage to make difficult decisions. Leadership is certainly not for the faint hearted!"
> – Gibson Sylvestre

> "Without belittling the courage with which men have died, we should not forget those acts of courage with which men have lived. The courage of life is often a less dramatic spectacle than the courage of a final moment; but it is no less a magnificent mixture of triumph and tragedy."
> – John F. Kennedy, Unites States President

8
LEAD WITH COURAGE

Great leaders are defined by the difficult decisions they make. Sadly, many leaders shy away from difficult decisions. They shy away because they want to avoid being wrong. However, the biggest mistake a leader can make is indecision. If you want to become a great leader you must be willing to make great decisions.

Leadership is all about having courage. Leadership is certainly not for the faint hearted. The German monk, Thomas á Kempis put it this way, "It is much safer to obey, than to govern." In other words, it is easier to be a follower than it is to be a leader. The leader is the one who is blamed at the end of the day. The leader is the first person to get to the office and is the last person to leave. President John F. Kennedy once declared, "Without belittling the courage with which men have died, we should not forget those acts of courage with which men have lived. The courage of life is often a less dramatic spectacle than the courage of a final moment; but it is no less a magnificent mixture of triumph and tragedy." A leader must be willing to sacrifice it all in order to do what is right, not what is convenient. Leadership is not about glamour it's about grit!

LIVE, STAND, AND DIE FOR WHAT YOU BELIEVE IN

A leader must stand up for what he or she believes in. Courage has convictions. Civil Rights leader Martin Luther King, Jr. was right when he said, "If you don't stand for something you'll fall for anything." It takes time to develop convictions. Every leader needs convictions. A man without convictions is not worth following! Author James Crooktest put it this way, "A man who wants to lead the orchestra must turn his back on the crowd." Leaders master the art of tuning out distractions.

In the 1960s President John F. Kennedy had to go against public opinion and do what was right for the nation in regards to the Civil Rights Movement. Kennedy wanted equal rights for African Americans and other minority groups in the United States. Many criticized the president; however, he went against the crowd and chose to be a courageous leader.

American author and humorist Mark Twain put it this way, "Whenever you find yourself on the side of the majority, it's time to pause and reflect." The famous Greek philosopher Socrates was a man of conviction. He made statements like, "The unexamined life is not worth living." It is said that Socrates uttered these piercing words at his heresy trials. Socrates came under scrutiny for his Socratic Method. The Socratic Method was a rhetorical strategy wherein one poses questions to expose the holes in a particular argument. He was on trial because many of the young men in Greece had accepted this method and began questioning the polytheistic philosophies of their day. In other words, Socrates encouraged his students to challenge the belief in many gods and wrestle with those beliefs until they could own their own beliefs. Simply put, Socrates was on trial for asking questions. Nevertheless, he stood for what he believed in. He lost the case and was sentence to death. All he had to do was recant his beliefs before the tribunal in Greece and he would have lived. Socrates stood by his beliefs and was killed for it. Many of us will never be asked to die for our convictions but if you were put on trial for your beliefs would you stand or defect?

> ...if you were put on trial for your beliefs would you stand or defect?

Former British Prime Minister Winston Churchill is a tremendous example of a courageous leader. When Hitler and his army threatened Europe and the world, Churchill rose to the occasion and accepted the challenge. In his memoir, Churchill wrote that despite the dangers that were in front of him, he possessed a cool, calm, confidence. "I felt," he wrote, "that I was walking with destiny, and that all my past life had been but a preparation for this hour and for this trial." He stood by his convictions. All of Great Britian was demoralized and in fear of the eminent danger. Churchill knew that the best way to approach a foe was not in fear but in fearlessness. Churchill told his sinister enemies, "We shall fight on the beaches, we shall fight on the landing ground, we shall fight in the fields and in the streets we shall fight in the hills; we shall never give up." Some historians say that Winston Churchill is credited for saving Western Civilization.

Leaders live by their beliefs...and in some cases when called upon will die by their beliefs. Courage is moving forward in the face of uncertainty, stress, pain, and fear. That's what leaders do, they defy the odds and keep moving!

WHY COURAGE IS CRITICAL TO A LEADER'S JOURNEY

1. Hardship Reveals Your Strengths And Your Courage

No one wants to follow a cowardly leader. When you go through a difficult challenge your strength as a leader is revealed. If you are immature; your immaturity will be revealed. If you are unprepared your lack of preparation will sabotage you. If you are a man or woman of character your character will be revealed. Author and business guru Bill George once said, "Like being in a crucible, a crisis tests whether you will hold fast to your beliefs." Some will sink, some will swim, courage is the deciding factor. A crisis either brings you down or brings you up. Courage brings you up and being a coward brings you down.

> *Courage brings you up and being a coward brings you down.*

2. Courage Gives You The Power To Reposition Yourself

Leaders get stuck in a rut but they don't stay in a rut. Every so often a leader must reposition his or herself to ascertain new opportunities. That is exactly what David Neeleman had to do. Neeleman was fired from Southwest Airlines. I'm sure he must have felt embarrassed and felt that his professional career was over. But Neeleman overcame his fears and decided to reposition himself from being an employee to being his own employer. In 1999 David Neeleman founded JetBlue. Today, JetBlue is one of the world's leading airlines. Neeleman learned the art of repositioning himself. If you don't like the way things are going, be brave and reposition yourself.

3. Courage Helps Leaders Face Reality

Sometimes leaders have to face brutal realities. We can either ignore our problems or explore our problems. When I say explore, I am speaking of exploring possible solutions to our problems. American novelist and civil rights activist James Baldwin once said, "Not everything that is faced can be changed. But nothing can be changed until it is faced." We must face the facts in order to lead effectively. Someone once said, "De-nial is not a river in Egypt." Leaders deal with reality not fantasy. If you have avoided an issue, deal with it today.

4. Courage Allows Leaders To Take Action

Transformative leaders have a bent towards action. Author and motivational teacher Denis Waitley put it this way, "The real risk is doing nothing." It takes courage to take action. You cannot sail the high seas from being on the shore. You have to go out and make something happen. You risk more with inaction than you do with taking action.

5. Courage Gives Us The Ability To Overcome Obstacles

In essence courage is the ability to overcome. Leadership is a perpetual act of overcoming. "There are two ways of meeting difficulties. You alter the difficulties, or you alter yourself to meet them," said U.S. President Woodrow Wilson. Choose to alter yourself to overcome your obstacles. We either overcome our obstacles or our obstacles will overcome us. "All of the great leaders have had one characteristic in common: it was the willingness to confront unequivocally the major anxiety of their people in their time. This, and not much else, is the essence of leadership," says Author and economist John Kenneth Galbraith.

> **We either overcome our obstacles or our obstacles will overcome us.**

6. Courage Keeps You Cool When Things Get Hot

In life things can heat up really quickly. When things get heated leaders stay cool. Most of the time people mimic leaders. If the leader freaks out, the people freak out. We must learn to keep our cool in the midst of tragedy. "The ability to keep a cool head in an emergency, maintain poise in the midst of excitement, and to refuse to be stampeded are true marks of leadership," said Professor R. Shannon. Learn to keep your composure in the midst of the storms of life.

COURAGE IS REVEALED IN TRAGEDY

Undoubtedly, adversity reveals who a man is to himself and it reveals the man to the world. September 11th, 2001 was one of the biggest tragedies in the history of the United States. Many innocent people lost their lives in a vicious terrorist attack in New York City as well as other cities. Shortly after the tragedy I traveled to the World Trade Center to help serve fire fighters and law enforcement officers as well as pay my condolences to several people who lost their loved ones.

Leadership requires bravery. Someone once said, "Noah was a brave man to sail in a wooden boat with two termites." How true. One leader who valiantly rose to the occasion was New York Mayor Rudolph Giuliani. Like Noah, he displayed his bravery when the odds were stacked against him. Instead of being crushed and paralyzed by the pressure he combined courage with compassion and moved quickly to help his fellow citizens.

Minutes after the terrorist attacks Mayor Giuliani was on the scene. He didn't quickly leave the city and run for cover. He wanted to be right in the middle of the pain to be available to comfort those panicking as well as give direction and information to fire fighters and police officers. Later that day in a press conference Mayor Giuliani would say to the people of New York, "Today is obviously one of the most difficult days in the history of the city. My heart goes out to all the innocent victims of this horrible and vicious act of terrorism. And our focus now has to be to save as many lives as possible." As I watched Mayor Giuliani from my television screen he appeared calm, cool, and resolute. The people of New York needed a strong, confident, and compassionate leader and Mayor Giuliani was exactly that, plus more. In addition, Mayor Giuliani would inspire the world by saying, "Tomorrow New York is going to be here. And we're going to rebuild, and we're going to be stronger than we were before... I want the people of New York to be an example to the rest of the country, and the rest of the world, that terrorism can't stop us..." That's exactly what the people of New York and the rest of the country needed to hear. In the midst of chaos and uncertainty the leader's most critical job is to comfort and restore confidence. Everyone watches the leader in times of crisis. They are watching to see if the leader will whine or shine. On September 11th Mayor Giuliani was definitely shining.

Leaders are forged in the crucible of affliction. And we saw a true courageous leader emerge out of that tragedy. The world has a great need for men and women to lead in these times of tremendous difficulty; will you be one of them? Will you dare to lay down your life for the wellbeing of others? Will you dare to be courageous?

> The world has a great need for men and women to lead in these times of tremendous difficulty...

COURAGE IN THE FACE OF FAILURE

Arthur Martinez saw the need for courage in both himself and his executives when he took over the failing Sears retail corporation. Martinez met with all of his senior management and explained just how enormously difficult the road ahead was going to be. He didn't paint some rosy fairytale picture. He was looking for men and women of great courage and grit. He assured them that the road ahead would be difficult, but "This is one of the greatest adventures in business history," he told his team. He wanted the stuff Winston Churchill and Abraham Lincoln were made of. Courage inspires us to work harder. Courageous leaders have the ability to inspire others in the midst of impossible situations. Later Martinez would say, "You have to be courageous, filled with self-confidence. If we do it, we'll be wealthier, yes. But more than that, we'll have this incredible psychic gratification. How can you not do it?" This is what I call contagious courage, the type of courage that inspires men and women to rise higher and achieve more. Because of his courage to lead in a time of turmoil Arthur Martinez earned the title, "The man who saved Sears." Are you ready to lead in the midst of danger and turmoil? If so, you will find your ranks amongst the world's brave and bodacious!

COURAGE AGAINST ALL ODDS

Fred Smith knows what it's like to succeed against all odds. Nobody believed in his vision except for himself. In 1962, while attending Yale University Smith outlined his audacious plans to create an overnight mail delivery service. At that point it was only a figment of his imagination. It all began with a college project that turned into an obsession. I call it a "college project gone wild!" In fact, when he turned in his project his professor scoffed at the viability of the project and gave the final pronouncement that what Smith was proposing was absolutely preposterous. What would you have done? Would you have given up? Most people would have. Not Fred Smith.

Smith mustered up all the courage he had and took decisive action on his dream. To prove his commitment he funded the new venture with his entire life savings. On June 18th, 1971, Smith founded Federal Express or FedEx, the world's first overnight express delivery company in the world. Smith risked it all...courage prevailed!

RUN TOWARDS YOUR GIANTS!

Courage is a source of power that activates resilience in the hearts and minds of leaders. The very thing you are running away from is the exact thing you should be running toward. The reality is great leaders are defined by the seemingly insurmountable mountains they conquer. So run towards your giants for your victory is closely linked with the risks you are willing to take. Courage is universally available to everyone who refuses to allow the pain of the past or the fear of the future to dictate their lives.

> *...great leaders are defined by the seemingly insurmountable mountains they conquer.*

STUDY GUIDE SECTION

KEY POINTS

While reading, What principles on having courage stood out to you the most? Why? Who is the most courageous leader you know? Why?

_____

_____

_____

REAL LIFE APPLICATION: PUTTING THE PRINCIPLES AND LESSONS INTO ACTION!

How will you apply this new information to your personal life?

_____

_____

_____

What are some obstacles that get in the way of you acting courageously as a leader? What are some practical steps you can take to help remove some of those obstacles? Who will you assign to keep you accountable?

_____

_____

PRACTICAL APPLICATION EXERCISE

Step 1- Write down a current decision that you are afraid of making.

Step 2- Write down at least seven ways you can overcome this fear.

Step 3- Pick one of the ways you wrote down and do it.

___

___

___

RATE YOURSELF

Overall, how well do you handle challenges as a leader?
(Check One Box Below)

Poor	Below Average	Average	Satisfactory	Excellent
1	2	3	4	5
❑	❑	❑	❑	❑

I am strongly committed to becoming a courageous leader.
(Check One Box Below)

Poor	Below Average	Average	Satisfactory	Excellent
1	2	3	4	5
❑	❑	❑	❑	❑

GROWING GOAL

Write down at least one goal/objective you have for becoming a courageous leader:

_____

_____

Stepping stone # 1

_____

_____

Stepping stone # 2

_____

_____

Stepping stone # 3

_____

_____

EPILOGUE

Leadership principles work for people who are willing to work the principles. It doesn't mater how many times you read this book, if you don't practice the principles it will not do you or anyone else any good. An average person who acts on principles outperforms a genius who simply reads and takes no action. This is an action oriented book and if you act upon these principles you will become a transformational leader. Things will begin to change and transform all around you.

Canadian economist John Kenneth Galbraith once said, "All of the great leaders have had one characteristic in common: it was the willingness to confront unequivocally the major anxiety of their people in their time. This, and not much else, is the essence of leadership." I want to challenge you to live life from the inside out, not the outside in. Feel what your people are feeling. Laugh with them. Cry with them. Don't go too far ahead of your people. A mentor of mine once told me, "When a general gets too far ahead of his troops, he's often mistaken for the enemy." Be with the people and of the people, yet at the same time be distinctive. Federal Express founder Frederick W. Smith, put it this way, "Leaders get out in front and stay there by raising the standards by which they judge themselves—and by which they are willing to be judged." Strive for excellence in all that you do. Refuse to allow your people to settle for less. Call your people higher; challenge them to live up to the amazing potential inside of them.

Leadership is a contact sport. At times it can be painful. The German monk Thomas á Kempis was right when he said, "It is much safer to obey, than to govern." In other words, it is easier to be a follower than it is to be a leader. However, we don't lead because it is easy, but because it's hard. We are called to serve others and that is our highest honor and our greatest joy. No matter what you do, leave a legacy that you are proud of. Make decisions that you will be proud of. As you think about what legacy you will leave as a leader think of this poem:

Your Name
You got it from your father,
it was all he had to give.
So it's yours to use and cherish,
for as long as you shall live.
If you lose the watch he gave you,
it can always be replaced.
But a black mark on your name, son,
can never be erased.
It was clean the day you took it,
and a worthy name to bear.
When he got it from his father,
there was no dishonor there.
So make sure you guard it wisely,
for when all is said and done,
You'll be glad the name is spotless,
when you give it to your son.
—Author Unknown

ABOUT THE AUTHOR

Author • Speaker • Leadership Consultant

Gibson Sylvestre is a dynamic and engaging speaker with a passion for reaching out and teaching others. He is the founder and president of GIBSON SYLVESTRE GLOBAL OUTREACH, a worldwide outreach organization.

He is also the CEO of INFINITE POSSIBILITIES INTERNATIONAL LLC, a marketing, training, and coaching boutique firm. Mr. Sylvestre has spent the last 15 years researching and learning the world's finest leadership, business, and personal development principles.

As a highly sought-after speaker he has had the honor of presenting in over 21 countries on five continents representing over 950,000 people worldwide. Whether Gibson is in Africa, India, Canada, Mexico, Europe, or Brazil, he carries a solid, no-fluff transformational massage. He is just as comfortable sharing his message with dignitaries, church leaders, students, civic leaders, business leaders, and television audiences. His message has proven to resound in the hearts of his many audiences.

In September 2007, he had the privilege of speaking at the "Values Voters Presidential Debate" in Fort Lauderdale, Florida. In addition, Gibson been endorsed by leading politicians, business moguls, top celebrity athletes, actors, church leaders, dignitaries, and many more.

Gibson incorporates humor into his presentations in order to engage his audiences while provoking them to think critically and dream big.

Gibson is the author of several life-changing books, including: *Life On Purpose, Supersize Your Life!, Staying Positive In A Negative World, Being A Promotable Person,* and *Leadership Sideways.*

A gifted communicator, Gibson is also the host of a radio program, "Your World, Your Impact," a 60-second feature encouraging listeners to impact their world for good. This radio program is heard daily by thousands of listeners across the state of Florida and Georgia.

Gibson is internationally known for his powerful, practical, and passionate style of sharing truth. Whether speaking in a stadium to an audience of thousands or one single person, he brings a message of true hope and peace. Gibson delivers customized, humorous, attention-getting, insightful, and informative world-class keynote speeches. He has the humor and energy of Robin Williams, the motivational power of Zig Ziglar, and the wisdom of Jack Canfield, all wrapped into one power-packed package. Your organization will be very grateful to have Gibson train, motivate, equip, and serve your people.

TO SCHEDULE SPEAKING APPOINTMENTS:

We facilitate first-class, customized, and relevant:
Corporate Trainings, Leadership Trainings,
Keynote Presentations, Motivational Teachings,
For bookings: www.gibsonsylvestre.com/bookings

OR VISIT US AT:
www.GibsonSylvestre.com

TO CONTACT US:
Online: www.GibsonSylvestre.com
MAIL Correspondence:
P.O. Box 934741, Margate, FL 33093
PHONE: 1-954-724-8455
Monday through Friday, 8:30 a.m.-6 p.m., EST